1968

may be

the changing world

Africa—the rebirth of self-rule

John Hatch

1967 OXFORD UNIVERSITY PRESS

Oxford University Press, Ely House, London W.1

GLASGOW NEW YORK TORONTO MELBOURNE WELLINGTON
CAPE TOWN SALISBURY IBADAN NAIROBI LUSAKA ADDIS ABABA
BOMBAY CALCUTTA MADRAS KARACHI LAHORE DACCA
KUALA LUMPUR HONG KONG TOKYO

By the same author:
The Dilemma of South Africa
New from Africa
Everyman's Africa
Africa—Today and Tomorrow
A History of Post-War Africa

FILMSET BY BAS PRINTERS LIMITED, WALLOP, HAMPSHIRE
PRINTED IN GREAT BRITAIN BY BILLING AND SONS LIMITED, GUILDFORD, SURREY

Preface

This short history has been written as an introduction to understanding modern Africa. It is deliberately selective. In each region emphasis has been laid on one or two particular stories. No attempt has been made to be comprehensive. Nor should significance be read into the selection of examples. It is not the author's intention, for instance, to suggest that the story of Kenya is more important than those of Tanzania or Uganda; that of Ghana more significant than Nigeria's. But it was thought that in the limited space available students would gain a better insight from reading one story thoroughly than by a shorter treatment of many histories.

Similarly, little will be found here about modern Arab Africa. The author rejects the common assumption that Africa can be divided politically, socially or economically by the Sahara; it was again simply shortage of space which dictated selection.

It will be noted that the general rule is to end each story at the moment of independence, though there are exceptions. This is deliberate. Africa's story is alive, changing every day. It is futile to try and chase it to keep a history book completely topical. Some general analysis of post-independence problems will be found in the last chapter.

Acknowledgements

The maps have been drawn by Regmarad.
We are grateful to the following for permission to reproduce photographs: Black Star: 22, photograph by Georg Gerster, by courtesy of Professor K. Michalowski, Polish excavations at Faras; 44b and c, 45f, 63e, 106a; British Museum: 11, 45d, 80; René Caillié: *Travels through Central Africa to Timbuctoo*: 24; Camera Press: 16, 28, 37, 46, 54, 58a, 67, 68, 74, 75, 92, 94, 95, 102, 119, 121, 127; J. Allan Cash: 30, 48, 50, 58b, 59d and e, 63a–d, 64, 74, 106b and c, 111, 112; Central Press: 57, 92; Bernard Fagg: 44a; Fox Photos: 56; The Gulbenkian Museum of Oriental Art, The University of Durham, England: 12; The Hull Museums: 36; Keystone Press Agency: 118; London Express News and Features Service: 73; Mansell Collection: 100; Paul Popper: 59c; Radio Times Hulton Picture Library: 53, 84, 98, 104; National Museum, Rhodesia: 20, 32; South Africa House: 21, 115; United Nations: 83; Society for the Propagation of the Gospel, photographs by Anthony Howarth: 106d and e, 114, 117; Trustees of the Wallace Collection, London: 45e; The White Fathers: 81; Roger Wood: 10, 13; Zambia Information Services: 90.

Contents

SAHARA DESERT

R. Niger

Lake Chad

R. Nile

S A V A N N A H

EQUATORIAL RAIN FOREST

Equator

CONGO BASIN

R. Congo

Lake Rudolf

DES

Lake Victoria

Lake Tanganyika

S A V A N N A H

Lake Malawi

R. Zambesi

Land over 3000 ft.

Swamps

KALAHARI DESERT

HIGH VELDT or GRASSLAND

Orange R.

Natural regions of Africa.

0   1000
Miles

1 Ancient Africa

Africa is a continent of variety. At present it is inhabited by about 300 million people. It covers one fifth of the world's land surface. Within it one could fit all Europe, the United States, India and Japan, yet still have room left. Some of its people have black skins, some brown, some pink, and there are many varying mixtures of these. They live in deserts, in dense rain forests, beside high snow-capped mountains, amongst wide stretches of grassland, near unhealthy swamps, on the shores of lakes, or in the midst of dusty, scrub, bush lands. Their continent has coastlines beside the Atlantic, the Mediterranean, the Red Sea and the Indian Ocean.

Africa is today divided into about fifty different countries. Nearly all of these countries are new, in the sense that their histories as nations began less than a hundred years ago. Their boundaries have usually been drawn by the European colonial powers which ruled them until recently. But African history goes back to the birth of the human race; so to understand Africa today, we have to trace the human story from its beginnings. Only so can we comprehend the variety of peoples who have grown up in this continent, how different types of them have come to live where they do now, and how their societies have grown into their present forms.

In this first chapter the words 'probably' and 'likely' appear often. This is because known facts are scarce, and historians have to base their accounts of the past on scanty evidence. In Africa most societies have not used writing to keep records. Evidence of ancient times is discovered by examining the rocks, unearthing old buildings, listening to folk tales, finding travellers' records; historians study all these varied remains and accounts of past societies and make their deductions as near to the truth as they can. New evidence often comes to light and historical theories may have to be changed. Nevertheless, we now have proof of human existence in Africa over the past two million years.

Africa, indeed, can claim to be one of man's birthplaces. It is generally accepted that man is distinguished from other animals by his ability to make and use tools. The earliest toolmakers yet discovered lived in the rocks of a gorge in Tanzania about two million years ago.

Here is one origin of human beings. There may be others. But during the thousands of generations since then various physical changes have occurred. They have been caused partly by different climates, partly through the effects of breeding. These changes have produced groups of men with similar features. We call them 'races'. Three racial types into which all human beings have been divided are the Negroid, the Caucasoid and the Mongoloid.

All the racial types have contributed to the development of Africa's peoples. The Caucasoids probably entered the continent from western Asia about 10,000 years ago and lived mainly in north and east Africa. Negro Africans are subdivided into Bushmen, Pygmies and 'true' Negroes. They developed out of older African types, adapting themselves to different circumstances. The Bushmen lived mostly in the east and south where the country was open. The Pygmies came from the forests of the Congo and Guinea. Some of their descendants still live by hunting and gathering plants in remote parts of central and south-western Africa. Nobody knows why they became such very small people, under 4 feet 6 inches. The 'true' Negroes probably came originally from the north of the equatorial forests at a time when there was much more rain in the Sahara region than there is today. They seem to have been fishermen, living a settled life by lakes and rivers. Mongols emigrated from Indonesia to Madagascar; later slaves from the same area came to southern Africa.

About two million years ago man first began to use tools.

Fifty thousand years ago he learnt how to use fire for heating and cooking. It is only about ten thousand years since he made his third great discovery—how to cultivate food crops.

Egyptian civilization

Again, the African continent provided one of the important chapters in this story. The great river Nile was the scene for one of man's first experiments in living together as a large-scale community. It seems likely that knowledge of how to cultivate crops and use animals for meat, milk, clothes, and haulage came to Africa from south-west Asia. Probably this knowledge was brought across the Suez Isthmus about five thousand years before the birth of Christ.

At first, between 5000 and 4000 B.C., communities using stone axes, hunting with bows and arrows, fishing with bone hooks, using pottery and weaving cloth, settled on the edges of the Nile valley. They learnt how to grow barley and wheat, storing it in sunken granaries lined with straw matting. Then, as these areas began to dry up and became desert, the people moved down into the river valley itself to clear swamps and jungle. The flood plains of the great river provided the ideal site in which to develop this early agricultural society. The river itself irrigated the area regularly during the flood seasons, leaving rich deposits of soil in the wake of its waters. Before long, flax and vegetable plants were added to the wheat and barley, whilst cattle, pigs, sheep and goats were domesticated.

The tremendous increase in food supplies grown in this new kind of society allowed the population to increase enormously. It has been estimated that at the beginning of this revolution, six or seven thousand years ago, there could not have been more than 20,000 people living in the valley. Two thousand years later the Nile community had grown to between three and six million.

Ancient Egyptian society lasted for some 4,000 years—about three times as long as Western European civilization has existed so far. Its early primitive villages grew into towns built of mud-walled, rectangular houses, with wooden doors and window frames. Large boats made from papyrus traded down the Red Sea, bringing back gold and copper from its shores. Craftsmen learnt how to shape alabaster jars and vases. Silver and lead were shipped from Mediterranean islands. Larger, wooden boats were built, using sixty oars, enabling the Egyptians to visit people developing similar societies in Mesopotamia.

As Egyptian society increased its store of knowledge, new arts, crafts and sciences developed. The Egyptians were amongst the first people to erect stone buildings, carve statues, build sea-going ships. They composed a solar calendar, used an alphabet, invented a form of writing. They devised new methods of irrigation, agriculture, engineering, metal working, manufacturing cloth, pottery, furniture and jewellery.

Egyptian skill in building can still be seen today in the survival of their royal tombs. The most notable of these, the pyramid of Gizeh, near Cairo, the tomb of the Pharaoh Khufur, was built 481 feet high, from about 2,300,000 blocks

The facade of the Great Temple of Ramases II at Abu Simbel; about 1330 B.C.

of stone, weighing an average
of two-and-a-half tons each,
and took 100,000 men twenty
years to erect. The ruins at
Luxor are a memorial to the
magnificence of the Egyptian
capital city, Thebes.

For the wealthy nobles,
priests and officials, Egyptian
life was comfortable and lei-
sured. They lived in brick and
wood houses; the rulers, called
Pharaohs, in luxurious palaces.
Gardens were walled to keep
the common people away,
swimming pools were built,
musicians and dancers enter-

Fowling scene from a painting on an Egyptian tomb;
about 1450 B.C.

tained, games, like draughts, were played, many servants
attended to the comfort of their masters.

All this luxury was possible because ways had been found for
individuals to produce more than the essentials needed by
themselves and their dependents. So some people could
accumulate wealth. But for the slaves, the peasants, the
ordinary people, life was usually hard, brutal, and short. They
even worshipped a different god from their masters, and
believed themselves destined for a less exalted future world.
Indeed, some of them were actually buried with their dead
masters to serve them in the next world.

The Egyptian contribution to European and Middle Eastern
civilizations has often been described. Persia, Greece and Rome
came to the Nile, learning as well as conquering. Much less is
known of Egypt's influence on the rest of the African continent.
Yet as new studies are made of African ruins and discoveries
made of various African societies, more is being learnt of the
influence of the Nile civilizations. It is becoming ever more
apparent that other African peoples contributed to Egyptian

11

life, whilst Egyptian civilization had a profound influence on societies growing elsewhere in the continent.

Travellers and merchants

The stories of travellers provide us with one source of knowledge. An explorer named Harkhuf was one of the earliest. More than two thousand years B.C. he led four caravan expeditions from Egypt southward, bringing back ebony, ivory and frankincense. On his fourth expedition he found an even greater prize, a 'dancing dwarf', clearly a pygmy from black Africa. When his Pharaoh heard the news he wrote to Harkhuf:

> Come northward to the court immediately; thou shalt bring this dwarf with thee, which thou bringest living, prosperous and healthy from the land of the spirits, for the dances of the god, to rejoice and (gladden) the heart of the king of the Upper and Lower Egypt, Neferkere, who lives forever.

The value which the Pharaoh placed on this rare man can be seen from his further instructions.

> When he goes down with thee into the vessel; take care lest he fall into the water. When (he) sleeps at night appoint excellent people, who shall sleep beside him in his tent; inspect him ten times a night. My majesty desires to see this dwarf more than the gifts of Sinai and of Punt.

This shows that Egyptians were trading with neighbouring African communities. At first trade was with small hunting groups. But references to Punt—which was either in Ethiopia or in Somalia on the Red Sea—show that at least one large trading centre also existed.

Indeed, Egyptian influence, through both trading and conquest, was affecting other African societies which were now becoming

Boxwood figure of a slave girl; Egyptian, about 1350 B.C.

states. One such was the kingdom of Kush, south of Egypt. This was situated in an area known as Nubia, part of today's Sudan. The Kushite kingdom is sometimes also known as Meroe, which was the name of its second capital.

Nubia produced immense quantities of gold. So Kush had the means to become very wealthy from the export of this metal, which even in those days was in much demand. The kingdom survived for over a thousand years, well into the Christian era. It became powerful enough to conquer Egypt and for a time dominated the ancient world. Through Kush, Egyptian civilization was taken into direct contact with black Africa.

Silver crown from Nubia ; about 500 B.C.

A famous Greek traveller, Herodotus, gave us a description of Meroe, the Kushite capital, on one of his journeys in Egypt in the fifth century B.C. He wrote:

> After the forty days' journey on land one takes another boat and in twelve days reaches a big city named Meroe, said to be the capital city of the Ethiopians. (He meant the Kushites.) The inhabitants worship Zeus and Dionysus alone of the Gods, holding them in great honour. There is an oracle of Zeus there, and they make war according to its pronouncements, taking from it both the occasion and the object of their various expeditions.

Herodotus also gave an interesting description of another African society of his time. The Phoenician trading states of the Near East had founded the city of Carthage in what is now Tunisia. Herodotus discovered that the Carthaginians

> . . . trade with a race of men who live in a part of Libya (Africa) beyond the Pillars of Heracles (the Straits of Gibraltar). On reaching this country, they unload their goods, arrange them tidily along the beach, and then, returning to their boats, raise a

13

smoke. Seeing the smoke, the natives come down to the beach, place on the ground a certain quantity of gold in exchange for the goods, and go off again to a distance. The Carthaginians then come ashore and take a look at the gold; and if they think it represents a fair price for their wares, they collect it and go away; if, on the other hand, it seems too little, they go back aboard and wait, and the natives come and add to the gold until they are satisfied. There is perfect honesty on both sides; the Carthaginians never touch the gold until it equals in value what they have offered for sale, and the natives never touch the goods until the gold has been taken away.

So far we have seen what was happening in north Africa during the several thousand years between the beginnings of Nile civilization and the birth of Christ. What was going on in the rest of the continent? In the plain belt between the Sahara and the rain forest, it seems likely that Negroes were learning the arts of agriculture at this time. They no doubt gained some knowledge from the Egyptians and Kushites, for there was some little trade across the Sahara. But their progress was much slower than that beside the Nile, for they were more isolated from other societies and had greater natural difficulties to overcome. In the east African highlands Caucasoid peoples were beginning to breed cattle and use them for food, transport and clothing. South of the equator there were very few people living. They still existed by hunting, gathering wild plants and fruits, and sometimes by trying to plant a few crops.

Iron age Africa

Then, shortly before the birth of Christ, the main African iron age began. Iron weapons appeared in Egypt as early as 666 B.C., wielded by Assyrian invaders. From about that time onwards the Phoenicians, the Kushites and the kingdom of Axum in Ethiopia all used iron. Its use may have spread along the trading routes across the Sahara to the Niger River and from the Nile to Lake Chad. Certainly several hundred years B.C. a civilization using iron was established in what is now central Nigeria. One theory is that after the Kushites were defeated by Axum some of their leaders fled westwards to the Lake Chad area and set up new states.

The use of iron spears enabled rulers and their armies to conquer weaker peoples and rule them within empires. Negro Africans, probably intermarried with migrants from northern Africa and speaking a language known as Bantu, began to move south. We shall call them Bantu peoples. They conquered the sparsely inhabited lands and set up new states. They were greatly helped in this by the appearance of new foods. Bananas and yams were brought from Asia to East Africa by traders and were found particularly suitable for cultivation in tropical Africa. They were added to the millet and rice crops native to the continent south of the Sahara and made it possible for larger populations than previously to be fed.

The Bantu peoples also took new forms of government with them. It may be that from Egypt through Kush had come the idea of a divine king ruling many people through a centralised government. Certainly for the first time many peoples in the heart of the continent were brought together in unified political units which we call states or empires. Sometimes members of these states broke away into rival, warring factions. This is the origin of what have often been called 'tribes'. They began to adopt special physical markings; some filed their teeth, others extracted particular teeth, some used facial scars to distinguish themselves from each other.

So by the time of Christ's birth Egyptian influence and the similar social habits of the Kushite state, Meroe, had spread westwards and southwards. The use of iron and copper enabled still more Africans to develop and adapt Egyptian–Kushite ideas. An increasing demand in Europe for gold stimulated trade across the Sahara between gold-producing west Africa and the Mediterranean. In return west Africans imported salt and manufactured goods from the north.

Kingdoms

In the fifteen hundred years after the birth of Christ many states grew out of this trade and the ability of rulers to conquer and govern. Ghana, Mali, Kanem, Songhai and a number of Hausa states rose to power in the west—though not with the same boundaries as the modern states of the same names. Each state had a monarch who was usually treated as a demi-god. The word 'ghana', for instance, originally meant 'divine ruler'. Sometimes these states would make war on each other. Mali, for example, eventually conquered Ghana in the thirteenth century A.D. They all demonstrated that their rulers had learnt how to organize large numbers of people into one society.

According to one account written in 1067,

> The king of Ghana can put two hundred thousand warriors in the field, more than forty thousand being armed with bow and arrow ... When he gives audience to his people, to listen to

A chief in Ghana with stool and insignia. Traditional ceremonies are still held (as is the coronation of a British Monarch) though the chiefs have lost their power.

their complaints and set them to rights, he sits in a pavilion around which stand ten pages holding shields and gold-mounted swords; and on his right hand are the sons of the princes of his empire, splendidly clad and with gold plaited into their hair.

The king was a divine ruler, believed by his subjects to draw his authority from supernatural sources. His state was based on kinship—the idea of inter-locking family circles. He had officials responsible to him and a treasury supplied from taxation. The strength of his state derived from its situation as a market. To the north there was a demand for gold to be sold to the Mediterranean and European world. There were also salt deposits there. Gold was mined in the south, where the people needed salt. States like Ghana, and its successors in neighbouring areas, thrived on the exchange of these commodities which took place in their cities.

The king (of Ghana) exacts the right of one dinar of gold on each donkey-load of salt that enters his country, and two dinars of gold on each load of salt that goes out.

The kingdom of Ghana existed during the period of European feudalism; it was certainly better ordered than many European states of its time. Its government was centralized around the king, who levied taxes. Most of its people were peasants, living on the land, or wandering pasturalists. It became strong through trade, the use of metal tools and the power of the king's army. Recent excavations on the site of what is believed to have been its capital city show that some of its wealthier people lived in considerable comfort. One house, built from a kind of slate on two storeys with a staircase, had nine rooms leading one to another, their walls decorated with yellow plaster. A large store of iron implements, lances, knives, nails, scissors, has been found, together with glass weights for weighing gold, pieces of pottery, and decorated stone.

In the central regions of the continent similar states also arose, organized to supply the demand for metals. In the Congo basin copper was mined and smelted. On the

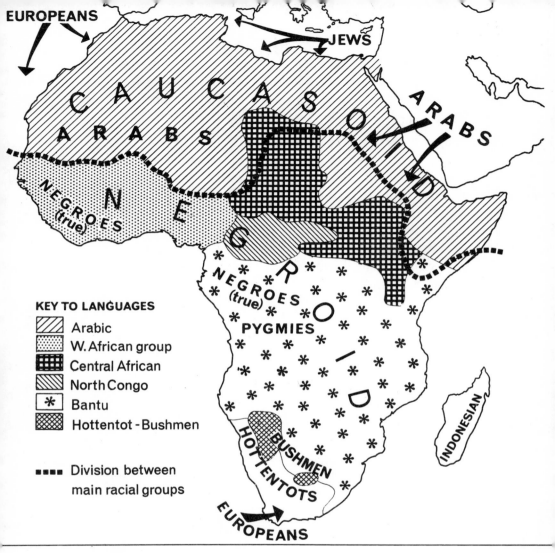

Main ethnic groups in Africa.

Rhodesian plateau gold was produced and exported. The ruins of Zimbabwe in Rhodesia remain today as evidence of a society probably dating back at least to the twelfth century and built by Bantu immigrants from the north.

In east Africa, within the great Rift Valley and its neighbourhood, conditions were different. Few of the metals sought by the world were found here. So there was not the same

18

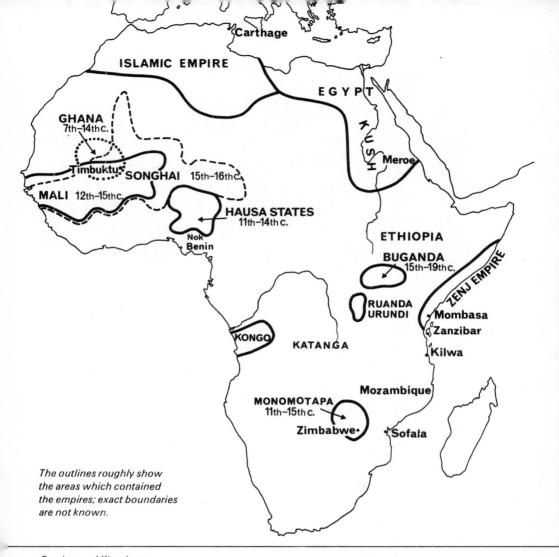

The outlines roughly show
the areas which contained
the empires; exact boundaries
are not known.

Empires and Kingdoms.

attraction to surmount the difficulties presented by the
swamps of the Upper Nile which barred contact with the
north. It was not until about the thirteenth century A.D. that
states and kingdoms began to emerge, at first in the region of
Uganda.

But on the coast, east Africa played a much more active rôle.
Egyptians explored along the Red Sea and down the Indian

19

Ruins at Nalatele 100 miles west of Zimbabwe (see page 30).

Ocean coastline several hundred years before Christ. Indeed, it has been reported that they sent a Phoenician expedition right round the continent as early as 600 B.C. Certainly from A.D. 45, when the monsoon winds were discovered, trade up and down this coast was constant. These convenient winds carry ships south-westward in December and north-east in March. They gave Arab, Indian and Chinese traders the opportunity to carry their cloth, porcelain and glass as far south as Zanzibar and Mozambique, returning north or east with iron, gold, ivory and slaves. By the seventh and eighth centuries A.D. references to black African slaves appeared in Arabia, Persia, Indonesia and China. There is even a story of a giraffe appearing early in the fifteenth century A.D. at a Chinese court. The winds are still used by Arabs to sail their ancient dhows, without compass or sextant, along the same coast.

This trade led to the building of coastal forts, cities and markets. It also led to much inter-marrying, particularly between Arabs and Africans, who thus created the Swahili people and developed the Swahili language. The principal city was Kilwa, one of the southern ports. It claimed authority over the others in what was called the Zenj empire, though each settlement kept considerable independence.

Kilwa thrived, like Ghana, on the proceeds of trade. Their rulers levied duties on the gold from Zimbabwe, the copper of Katanga, the iron, ivory and slaves which passed through their markets; similarly, tribute was taken from the Asian traders who brought their goods to exchange for these African products. The east African city states were also ruled by kings, but, according to one account written in the tenth century A.D., 'once he (the king) be-

Rock painting by bushmen in South Africa.

comes tyrannical and departs from the rules of justice, they cause him to die and exclude his posterity from succession to the throne . . .'. Another writer, in the fourteenth century A.D., described Kilwa as 'one of the most beautiful and well-constructed towns in the world. The whole of it is elegantly built. the roofs are built with mangrove poles.' The same writer describes most of Kilwa's inhabitants as jet-black in colour, and with tattoo marks on their faces.

The rest of the continent—most of southern Africa—was inhabited at this time only by scattered groups. They still lived by hunting and collecting wild plants or fruits. It was here that the Bushmen were driven by the southward advance of the Bantu and the Caucasoid peoples from the east. Some of the Bushmen inter-married, probably with east African Caucasoids, to produce the Hottentots, who lived in south Africa.

A number of external influences affected African development over these centuries. Egypt not only experienced occupation from Greeks and Romans. For a time it was overrun by Semitic tribes. Later many Jews settled in various parts of north Africa. Christianity appeared during the

Madonna and Child with Nubian prince, between eighth and tenth centuries A.D.

Roman period. It spread through North African societies and into the Sudan and Ethiopia, assisted by the fine Roman system of communications. One of the most famous Christians, St. Augustine, was a Libyan Berber from Carthage.

There is evidence, too, of frequent migrations of peoples from Arabia and other parts of the Middle East into north Africa. They almost certainly introduced the camel into Africa. This animal, used for riding and carrying loads, led to the growth of wandering nomadic groups who raided the settled agricultural communities. In the fifth century A.D. north Africa was also invaded by the Germanic Vandals, though they were defeated in the following century by the Byzantines.

Thus Africa during this period witnessed a constant movement of peoples, the appearance of many new communities and ideas, the growth and decline of societies. The last major influence of the times was the arrival of the Islamic religion. The prophet Mohammed, born at Mecca near the Red Sea in A.D. 570, gave the Arabs a religious faith which united their rival factions. It also inspired them with a desire to spread their faith to other peoples, if necessary by conquest. They invaded Egypt in A.D. 639, conquered the whole of the African north coast and crossed into Spain. For the next thousand years Islam dominated north Africa and gradually extended its ideas both across the Sahara and down the east coast. But before that millenium ended new and even more powerful invaders had entered the continent.

2 Europe seizes Africa

During the first 600 years after the time of Christ Christianity spread through most of north Africa. But its roots did not sink very deep. The militant advance of Islam soon after the death of Mohammed in A.D. 632 drove it out of almost all Africa except Ethiopia. A hundred years later followers of Islam had swept across north Africa to the Atlantic. They then crossed into Spain, only being halted at the Pyrenees.

For the next 500 years political and religious wars disrupted life in northern Africa. They often enlarged the desert by destroying irrigation and agriculture. They also undermined some of the African states south of the Sahara, causing Negro peoples to migrate again.

Yet Muslim Arabs brought new arts and culture to northern Africa. The Islamic idea of one God and brotherhood amongst

Trade routes used by the Arabs.

Timbuktu—a print made in 1830.

believers was combined with a technical knowledge, including many of the navigational skills which were later to be used by Europeans to explore the oceans. So in northern and north-western Africa mosques and schools were built, whilst scholars from other lands visited these centres of learning. Timbuktu became one of the greatest commercial and learned cities of the medieval world. At the beginning of the sixteenth century one visitor wrote:

> Here in Timbuctu there are great store of doctors, judges, priests and other learned men, bountifully maintained at the king's cost and charges. And hither are brought divers manuscripts or written books out of Barbary, which are sold for more money than any other merchandise.

Islam influenced east Africa later than the north and west. From the middle of the thirteenth century to the end of the fifteenth most of the east coast was brought under Islamic influence. This was the period in which Islam was also spreading through Asia to India and Indonesia (whence migrants had already settled in Madagascar). The Muslims built towns of stone down the east coast. These prospered through the extension of trade to Asia and were enriched by Muslim culture. Gold and copper from Rhodesia and Katanga continued to be exported, along with ivory and slaves. These were exchanged for the cloths, spices and even Ming porcelain of Arabia, India and China.

Organized states had already developed in the east African interior, around the great lakes, and particularly in Uganda. But there seems to have been no trade between them and the coast. They were cut off from the market ports by a belt of arid, infertile land discouraging trading caravans.

European traders

It was from the rivalry between Muslims and Christians that Europe came into closer contact with Africa than ever before. In medieval Europe at this time, the wealthy classes continually demanded goods which could only be found in Asia. These included spices, for flavouring meat preserved in salt all winter, sugar, silks, drugs, perfumes and ivory. They were brought by merchants to the eastern Mediterranean, where Italian city traders bought them to distribute through Europe. The Muslims controlled the trade as far as the Mediterranean, whilst the Venetians had established a monopoly in the Mediterranean itself. During the fifteenth century, the rising power of the Ottoman Turks in Asia Minor and Egypt threatened to cut the life-line of this vital trade between Asia and Europe.

So some European merchants began to seek new routes from Europe to Asia in order to avoid these restrictions and to cut costs. The Portuguese were the first to succeed. They and the Spaniards concentrated at first on driving the Islamic Moors out of their peninsula. Then they followed them across into

A simplified plan taken from a medieval map of the world.

Morocco, but they never succeeded in conquering that country.

The son of the king of Portugal, who came to be known as Henry the Navigator, learnt much from the Arabs encountered in north Africa. He heard of the gold coming from south of the Sahara, that Arabs navigated down the east African coast, that some of them believed the continent to be surrounded by oceans. This was heresy to medieval Europe, which believed the world to be flat, with Africa stretching to the southern most edge.

Henry collected these ideas in his geographical academy. He hired marine engineers to design and build ships able to sail against the wind and fitted for ocean exploration; cartographers to draw new maps; scientists to develop the compass; and sailors with the courage to brave the mysterious Atlantic. He believed that if he could organize Portuguese expeditions down the west coast of Africa he could enrich his country with the gold of Guinea, perhaps with the spice trade of Asia. At the same time he hoped to outflank Islam.

From 1415 onwards, despite many fears and mutinies,

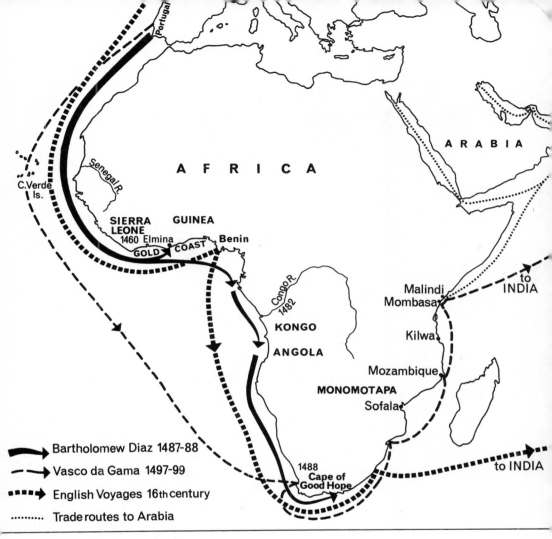

Key:

▬▶ Bartholomew Diaz 1487-88

--▶ Vasco da Gama 1497-99

▪▪▪▶ English Voyages 16th century

········ Trade routes to Arabia

Map labels: Portugal, C.Verde Is., Senegal R., SIERRA LEONE, GUINEA, 1460 Elmina, GOLD COAST, Benin, AFRICA, Congo R. 1482, KONGO, ANGOLA, ARABIA, to INDIA, Malindi, Mombasa, Kilwa, Mozambique, MONOMOTAPA, Sofala, 1488 Cape of Good Hope, to INDIA

Voyages of discovery and trade routes.

Portuguese sailors edged their way down Africa's west coast. In 1441 they brought back the first Negroes. In 1443 they found their first gold dust. The following year they reached the Cape Verde islands. These they brought under Portuguese rule as a base for trade up the river Senegal. In 1459, the year before his death, a secret map was made in Venice for Henry. It showed Africa with a southern tip around which ships could sail.

27

A bronze plaque of a Portuguese soldier made in Benin, probably seventeenth or eighteenth century.

The voyages continued after Henry's death. They reached the Gold Coast in 1471. Eleven years later the Portuguese built the fort of Elmina to defend their monopoly over the rich gold deposits they found there. The fort can still be visited in Ghana today. It was eventually completed with the consent of local Africans; but, at first, the building of the fort caused some fears which were later to recur in other parts of the continent. One chronicler writes:

The Negroes, upon seeing the destruction and utter ruin of their sacred rocks, meanwhile believed that they were looking upon the loss of all hope of their salvation, and all eagerly and in a great rage took up their arms and struck so hard at the workmen, who, not being able to resist them, retreated in flight to the boats.

The Portuguese also visited the city state of Benin in Nigeria. 'Its houses are made of mud walls covered with palm leaves,' wrote one visitor. Here they found plentiful supplies of pepper which they began to export back to Europe. Then they found another well-organized state at the mouth of the Congo. In 1488 Bartholomew Diaz was accidentally blown round the Cape to find his ship in the Indian Ocean. Another Portuguese explorer made his way to India through Egypt and sailed from there in an Arab dhow down the east African coast. The climax of exploration was reached when, between 1497 and

1499, Vasco da Gama took an expedition from Portugal right round Africa, up the east African coast, across to India and back again. He brought back a cargo of spices from India. One of Henry's dreams had come true.

One of Henry's objectives was to convert Africa's peoples to Christianity. Yet as soon as Africans were taken back to Portugal, some of the Portuguese merchants saw the chance of making a profit out of them. Labour was short on many Portuguese farms. Africans sold as slaves would bring a good price. So Henry's evangelistic intentions were soon transformed into the start of the European–African slave trade.

The change in the objectives of the Portuguese can be seen in their relations with the Kongo kingdom. Portuguese sailors encountered this large, well-ordered state of about two-and-a-half million inhabitants in 1482. Its people, the Bakongo, were particularly skilful smiths, forging weapons for hunting and warfare. The king ruled through chiefs and sub-chiefs whom he appointed to govern the various provinces. Around the state's boundaries were groups of smaller states, each under a Bakongo ruler owing theoretical allegiance to the Kongo king. One of these rulers was given the hereditary title of 'Ngola', from which came the name of the later Portuguese colony, Angola.

The Bakongo received the Portuguese in a friendly manner. The king and his wife agreed to become Christians. Their son went to Portugal with other young men to be educated. He was baptized and consecrated as the first African bishop. The next king, Affonso, ruled as a Christian from 1507 to 1543. Missionaries, stonemasons, builders and other skilled workers were sent out from Portugal. Large quantities of stone were also shipped. The capital, named San Salvador, was rebuilt with fine churches and palaces.

It was the desire of Portugal's merchants for slaves which destroyed this Christian effort. In the sixteenth century the demand for labour in Portugal's new American colony, Brazil, offered still more lucrative opportunities to the slave traders. King Affonso even wrote to the king of Portugal in

Fort Jesus built by the Portuguese at Mombasa.

1526 asking that he

> ... should not send here either merchants or wares, because it is our will that in these Kingdoms there should not be any trade of slaves nor outlet for them.

Again, in the same year, he complained that many of his own people were being tempted by Portuguese wares to

> ... kidnap even noblemen and the sons of noblemen, and our relatives, and take them to be sold to the white men who are in our Kingdoms; ... as soon as they are taken by the white men they are immediately ironed and branded with fire.

The Portuguese king, however, did not stop the slave trade. Instead, from 1575 for the next century, Portugal waged a war of conquest south of the Kongo kingdom. Bands of Africans were armed to attack surrounding peoples to supply slaves for the trade to Brazil. Eventually, Kongo itself became involved. In 1660 the state was defeated by the Portuguese and it broke up. Angola remained the main supply centre for her slave trade, being devastated by its effects.

Meanwhile, the Portuguese set about establishing a monopoly over the rich trade of the Indian Ocean. They captured most of the Arab trading stations on the east African coast and set up headquarters at Mozambique. From here they established a trading link to their new colony of Goa, on the west coast of India, and across to the East Indies. But they never gained a firm hold on the east African coast. In 1593, to try and quell opposition, they built at Mombasa the great citadel of Fort Jesus. Yet the Arabs still secured support from Arabia.

Portuguese hopes of the gold trade were also soon shattered. Conflict with the Arabs, which caused the disruption of the Arab caravan trade, proved fatal. Gold exports, which had depended on the caravan traffic, almost disappeared. By the end of the eighteenth century the Arabs had driven out most of the Portuguese and re-established their dominance over the east coast.

Yet the efforts of the Portuguese in east Africa had one interesting result. Finding that the gold trade was dwindling, they sent expeditions up the Zambezi to seek the source of gold itself. Here they encountered the state of Monomotapa in Southern Rhodesia. This seems to have been the kingdom which occupied the royal village and temple at Zimbabwe from about the eleventh to the fifteenth centuries. Its people said that they had moved northwards because they had exhausted their salt supplies. At the time that the Portuguese found them they ruled the whole of the Zambezi valley from Kariba to the sea, together with wide stretches of Southern Rhodesia and Mozambique. A Dominican priest who visited the Monomotapa area at the end of the sixteenth century described the gold thus:

It is found in poulder like sand; in graines like beads; in pieces some smooth as they were melted, others branched with snags, others mixed so with Earth, that the Earth being well washed from them, they remayne like Honiecombes; those holes before full of red Earth, seeming as though they were also to be turned into Gold.

The tower was built about 1700 but other ruins at Zimbabwe date from about A.D. 1200

Today we can still see the ruins of Zimbabwe and other stone buildings in surrounding areas. But at the end of the seventeenth century the Monomotapas, undermined by subjection to the Portuguese and by the slave trade, were driven out of their lands by another African state. The Portuguese were also expelled.

In the meantime, Portugal had been followed to the west African coast by rival European maritime nations. For about a hundred years after her first explorations Portugal was able to maintain almost a monopoly there. She established coastal bases to which Africans brought gold dust, slaves and pepper in exchange for cloth, metal implements and firearms. Many Portuguese officials married African wives, so that the settlements became both European and African.

This monopoly was helped by Spain's interest in America and the Pope's division of the newly-discovered lands between Spain and Portugal. The West Indies and most of America were given to Spain; Africa and Asia to Portugal.

But towards the end of the sixteenth century other Atlantic states began to covet the wealthy trade of Portugal and Spain. Holland, Sweden, Denmark, Germany, France and Britain all refused to accept the Pope's ruling. Desire to share in the new trade brought conflict between Atlantic Europe and the Roman church; it provoked war against the Iberian states.

In the sixteenth century the French and British defied the Portuguese and tried to trade with west Africa. In the seventeenth century the Dutch and British broke Portugal's monopoly of the Indian Ocean. In the same century French, British and Dutch attacked Spanish power across the Atlantic.

By now the Atlantic Ocean, as a way to America and Asia, had replaced the Mediterranean as the focal area of world power. Already, one of the main cargoes it carried was slaves. They were taken from west Africa to the silver mines of Mexico or to the sugar plantations of the West Indian islands. By the middle of the seventeenth century the Dutch had captured control of the trade in west Africa from the Portuguese, though Portugal continued to send slaves from Angola to Brazil. By the end of the century France and Britain had reduced Dutch power. The eighteenth century saw a struggle for supremacy in the Atlantic between these two nations. It was eventually won by the British.

Slavery

The slave trade dominated relations between Africa and Europe from the beginning of the sixteenth to the end of the nineteenth centuries. Most of the effects on Africa were destructive, though it brought some developments too. Some missionaries did useful work. The new trade routes brought fresh ideas and new goods to Africa. Some African societies were brought into contact with each other for the first time.

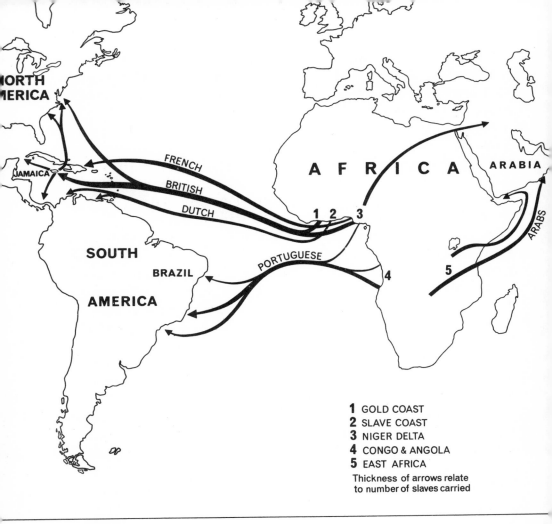

Slave routes.

Important new tropical foods, like cassava, maize and sweet potatoes, were introduced. Certain African states, Oyo, Benin, Dahomey and Ashanti in the west, flourished from their trade with Europeans, though each was eventually to be undermined by its dependence on the slave trade.

Slavery itself had been common in Africa, Asia and Europe from early in human history. But there were two kinds of slavery. In the first, criminals, rebels or prisoners of war were taken from their own family groups and attached to other families as compulsory servants. They might be bought and sold in this process. But they were treated as human beings, allowed to marry and become part of their new family household. This is called 'domestic' slavery, and was usual in Africa. In Europe, Arabia and most of Asia slavery usually had an economic motive and is known as 'economic' or 'chattel' slavery. It was based on the desire to secure labour. The slave became an absolute possession of his master.

The result of the meeting of these two kinds of slavery was disastrous for Africa. The Africans at first saw no difference between selling slaves to the Europeans and Arabs and to other Africans. The Europeans found that they could make large profits by exchanging copper, iron, cloth and firearms for these slaves, whom they could then sell as labourers across the Atlantic. European nations on the Atlantic coast became rich from the produce grown by the slaves on the American or Caribbean plantations. The revolution in ship building needed to provide the new types of slave ships and new navies to fight their competitors gave them great naval power.

But the Africans did not anticipate the kind of slavery which the Europeans imposed. There are many descriptions of the terrible conditions in which African slaves were shipped across the Atlantic and Indian Oceans. An Englishman, Walsh, in 1829 in the frigate North Star, described the scene he saw in a slaver. The cargo consisted of 505 men and women—55 had died and been thrown overboard during 17 days at sea.

> Slaves were all enclosed under grated hatchways, between decks. The space was so low that they sat between each other's legs, and stowed so close together, that there was no possibility of lying down, or at all changing their position, by night or by day. As they belonged to, and were shipped on account of different individuals, they were all branded like sheep, with the owners' marks of different forms. These were impressed under their breasts, or on their arms, and, as the mate has informed me with perfect indifference, burnt with a red hot iron . . .

Embarking slaves—a nineteenth century lithograph.

Although many Africans throughout the continent continued to supply slaves to the markets, the way in which millions of African slaves were treated could only have the long-term effect of embittering relations between Africans and Europeans. In Africa itself chaos resulted. Many millions of men, women and children (estimates vary widely from 10 to 50 million) were torn away from their homes. The new European firearms, bought with slaves and used to capture more slaves, provoked widespread warfare across the continent. Kingdoms rose and fell, well-ordered societies were destroyed and the comparatively peaceful growth of medieval Africa was brought to a disastrous halt.

During the nineteenth century attempts to abolish the slave trade played another important part in relations between Africa and Europe. By the start of the century Britain, in particular, was fast becoming an industrial society. The sugar magnates of the West Indies were losing political power. The new manufacturers looked to Africa as a market in which to sell their manufactured goods in exchange for the raw materials needed for industry. The slave trade stood in the way.

Meanwhile, some Europeans had become uneasy over slavery. The Christian church had condemned it, but done little to obstruct it. Now churchmen and humanitarians began to campaign against both slavery and the slave trade. By 1787 a new colony called Sierra Leone was founded in west Africa as a home for slaves freed by law in Britain. In 1822 the Americans established Liberia for a similar purpose.

Denmark outlawed the slave trade in 1804; Britain in 1807; America in 1808; and Holland in 1814. British naval power was used to stop others continuing it, though this took most of the rest of the century. In 1833 slavery itself was declared illegal throughout British possessions.

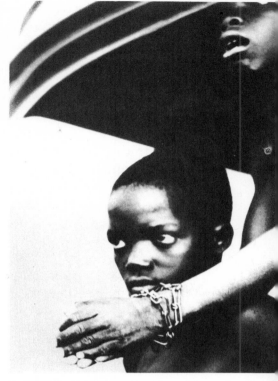

In 1964 these children were found in a slave caravan in Chad on the way to an Arab market.

Missionaries and explorers

In this early part of the nineteenth century Europeans still knew very little about the interior of Africa. The slave trade had depended on Africans bringing their captives to markets on the coast. But before the end of the eighteenth century some attempts had been made by Europeans to discover what lay within the continent. Missionaries and traders together saw that the interior of Africa was explored during the next hundred years.

Christian churches began to feel a duty to convert pagan Africans. They sent missionaries who took with them education and medicine as well as the Bible. Some of the missionary societies were also associated with geographic exploration. David Livingstone was both a missionary and an explorer. So were some of the Germans who took part in these exploits.

This was a time when colonies had become generally unpopular. Trade was the main objective and in the period of 'free trade' colonies were thought to be an unnecessary expense and a restriction on commerce. Livingstone's own prescription for Africa was 'Christianity and commerce', which he thought would drive out the slave traders. The search for trade and the Christian quest for souls took Europeans into the heart of west, east and central Africa. South Africa, as we shall see later, had been settled by Europeans from the middle of the seventeenth century. During this same nineteenth century period of exploration they also explored more of their country.

European occupation

This anti-colonial phase lasted only until the fourth quarter of the nineteenth century. The economic and military needs of European nations changed. United Germany appeared on the European scene for the first time. She presented a direct challenge to the industrial, commercial and military power of Britain and France. And the new tensions which developed in Europe were reflected in competition for African colonies. Within a few years all Europe became convinced that national and international power depended on possessing an empire. Economic, military and political imperialism became the fashion until it began to be questioned after the 1914–18 War.

In 1880 the French held Algeria and Senegal, Britain the Gold Coast and the Cape Colony. The Turks retained a nominal suzerainty over Tunis, Tripoli and Egypt. But Europeans controlled only coastal areas in the rest of the continent. These consisted of places like Gambia, Sierra Leone, Lagos, Gabon, Angola and Mozambique. Yet by the end of the

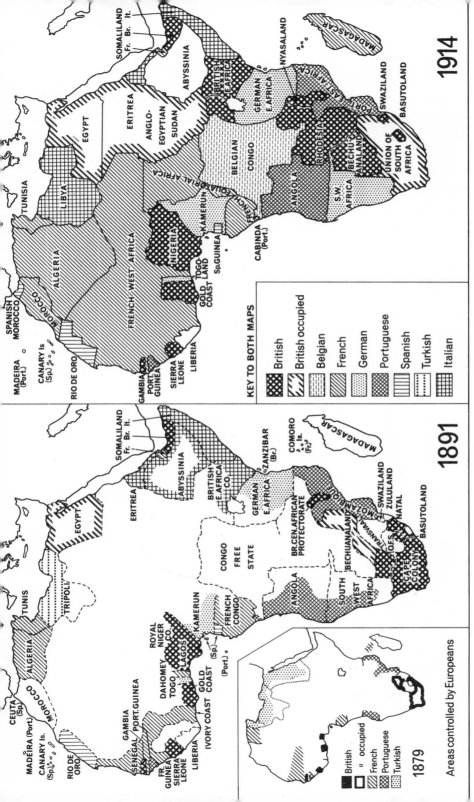

European control over Africa grows.

century virtually the whole continent had been divided between European powers.

King Leopold II of Belgium was the first to take advantage of the explorations. From 1876 onwards he established a personal commercial empire south of the Congo river. The British became the actual, though not the legal, rulers of Egypt from 1882. Then, between 1883 and 1888, the Germans laid claim to South-West Africa, Togoland, the Cameroons and east Africa.

A conference was held in Berlin in 1884–5 to discuss these rival ambitions. To prevent indiscriminate claims it was agreed that the qualification for declaring a 'sphere of influence' should be effective occupation of a territory. Thereafter, agents of all colonial powers roamed African territories, their pockets bulging with treaty forms. They persuaded African chiefs to affix their marks to them for the price of a few trinkets, alcohol or firearms. Great stretches of land, which no chiefs really owned, thus passed into European hands. The Europeans believed that they owned this land; to the Africans this was inconceivable, for the land belonged permanently to the tribes. They thought they had leased the use of the land. Trading companies were formed to exploit the newly-opened commerce. The treaty merchants then called on their governments to send officials and troops to defend the territory acquired.

The French moved eastward from Senegal and northward from Gabon, the expeditions meeting at Lake Chad. The British expanded northwards from the Cape through Bechuanaland to the Zambezi, led by Cecil Rhodes' British South Africa Company. They also marked out a sphere of influence in east Africa in what is now Kenya, with an option on Uganda. Later they laid claim to Northern Rhodesia and Nyasaland. The Italians occupied Eritrea and Somalia. Frontiers throughout the continent were negotiated by European statesmen in European capitals according to purely European interests and balances of power. The political boundaries drawn around the new colonies had no relation to anything African; they frequently fragmented tribes, cut up economic regions, divided geographic units.

In the early years of the twentieth century the British defeated the Boers and annexed all South Africa; Morocco was partitioned between France and Spain; whilst the Italians conquered Libya.

This European partition of the African continent was not accomplished without opposition. The Islamic hero Samori fought the French in the western Sudan. The Ashanti in the Gold Coast, the Mahdi in the Sudan, the Matabele in Rhodesia, battled against the British. The Ethiopians actually defeated the Italians.

Yet, by 1914, when the same European powers whose rivalry had divided Africa finally went to war, only Liberia and Ethiopia remained free from European rule. The African continent was now a patchwork of colonies governed from London, Paris, Brussels, Lisbon, Rome, Madrid and Berlin.

3 West Africa

The Europeans who began to govern African colonies at the end of the nineteenth century held certain important beliefs. This was particularly true of the British, but it applied also to the French, Belgians, Germans and Italians. Europeans believed that the tremendous technical discoveries of their continent during the nineteenth century had given them the secret of progress. They considered that theirs was the greatest civilization ever known. It gave them a deep sense of superiority and self-righteousness. They considered their society to be a universal ideal, created from natural laws. And this European society was essentially expansionist. It built railways in America, organized commerce in India and China, provided shipping lines to Australia, and lent money everywhere. Though for most of the century Britain was opposed to actual annexation of new colonies, nevertheless her people believed in persuading the world to follow her paths, and she kept a powerful navy to make sure that the persuasion was successful. Palmerston, the mid-nineteenth century British Foreign Secretary, expressed this spirit when he declared:

> . . . commerce may go freely forth, leading civilization with one hand, and peace with the other, to render mankind happier, wiser, better. Sir, this is the dispensation of Providence.

On another occasion he revealed his ideas of the part that the government should play in this providential plan.

> It is the business of government to open and secure the roads for the merchant.

British objections to the annexation of colonies disappeared towards the end of the century as the conditions of international

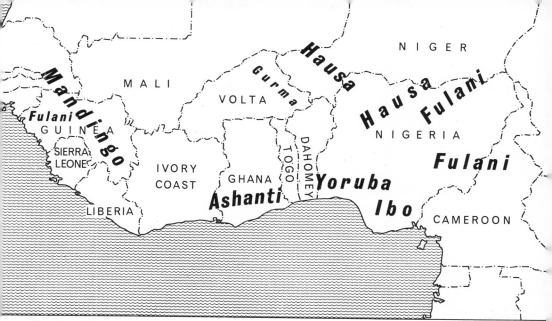

Peoples and countries of West Africa.

trade changed. But colonization only added political control to already existing economic domination.

The British and other European peoples who actually took responsibility for their new African subjects had been brought up in the atmosphere of European superiority. Africa was not in the mainstream of international commerce; but the new European colonists assumed that they should bring Africans into their 'enlightened' world by teaching them to follow the European example.

At this time almost no Europeans knew anything of Africa's past. They knew nothing of the Nigerian pre-Christian Nok terra cotta figures nor of the bronze art of Benin and Ife. Nor had they heard of the African empires which flourished before Europeans came to the continent. They believed all Africans to be primitive, ignorant savages. So the European rulers felt justified in ruling their new subjects, if necessary for centuries, in order to develop the natural resources of Africa and lead its peoples to a European-type civilization.

But although this was a general attitude amongst the Europeans, the policies adopted by the colonial powers were

43

a   b

not identical. West Africans were particularly affected by the differences between the colonial policies of France and Britain. The French believed that the finest thing they could do for Africans was to make them into black Frenchmen. So, from the middle of the nineteenth century, Africans from the coastal towns of Senegal could become French citizens. This meant that they were subject to the laws of France and entitled to send members to the French parliament in Paris. But as French rule spread into the interior of Africa it was thought that the more remote inhabitants would not understand French customs. They were left under their traditional laws, though governed by a pyramid of French officials, with the Governor-General in Dakar at the top. The French nevertheless hoped that eventually even the most remote communities would be influenced by education, Christianity and commerce to become citizens of France.

The British, in contrast, always remembered that the Americans had broken from the British Empire because they were not allowed self-government. British policy in her principal colonies, Australia, New Zealand, Canada and South

44

d

e

West African Sculpture
- (a) Terracotta head from Nok, Nigeria; between 300 B.C. and 200 A.D.
- (b) Head of Terracotta from Ife, Nigeria; about twelfth century
- (c) Terracotta head from Ife; about fifteenth century
- (d) Bronze head from Benin, Nigeria; about sixteenth century
- (e) Gold trophy head from Ghana, of a Northern King defeated in battle about 1830
- (f) Bronze figures from Ife; about sixteenth century

f

Woman from Dakar in French West Africa.

Africa, was to allow the inhabitants increasing self-government. Policy in Africa was similar, though self-government was much more restricted.

The government of each British African colony was separate. Each had its governor, responsible to the British government. He had an executive council of his officials to advise him. Each colony also had a legislative council, eventually with limited powers to make laws. The earliest legislative council in west Africa was set up in Gambia in 1843; the Gold Coast followed in 1850; Lagos in 1862; Sierra Leone in 1863.

At first, the members of these legislative councils were British officials. Then a few British missionaries and traders were added. Later, educated Africans were also nominated.

The legislative council was a kind of infant parliament. Some form of self-government could grow out of it, as in the white-settled colonies like Canada or Australia. The British assumed that this would take so long that they hardly thought about it. But the separate councils for making colonial laws illustrated the contrast with the French idea of bringing all African subjects into a Greater France.

Before the Europeans could rule effectively, however, they had to assert their authority over the huge area of west Africa. Frontier lines could be drawn on maps, but it was many years before the colonial officials themselves could cover the vast lands stretching inland from the coastal bases. The French alone claimed a west African empire of some 1,800,000 square miles, nine times the size of France herself.

Nor were the Africans of the interior willing to accept European rule passively. It took the French from 1854 to 1865 to conquer Senegal. Military operations in Guinea and Ivory Coast lasted until 1915. Many of the desert nomadic tribes resisted even longer. The Ashanti in the Gold Coast fought a series of wars against the British. They were finally conquered only in 1901. It was not until five years later that the Muslim Fulani emirs of northern Nigeria capitulated.

There were other difficulties for the European colonial officials to meet. For a long time they had the task of ruling peoples divided into many tribes and scattered over vast areas. Their home governments expected them to provide themselves with the money to pay for their administration. Few Africans earned enough money for taxes, whilst trade was never sufficient to supply adequate revenues.

For these reasons both British and French officials, despite their different outlooks, began to use African chiefs to assist in administration. Friendly chiefs who would collect taxes had their local authority supported by the colonial officials. Sir Frederick (later Lord) Lugard, became best known for this method of 'indirect rule' which he initiated in northern Nigeria. But the practice became widespread throughout west Africa. Although it helped understaffed colonial governments, it also gave extra powers to traditional African rulers who were often strongly opposed to new ideas.

The period between the two world wars, after colonial rule had been entrenched, was comparatively quiet in west Africa. Most of the Africans continued to live in their mud and thatched hut villages. They grew a few crops, kept some chickens, worked at various handicrafts. Laws were few, though local customs were strong; and life was less complicated than in an industrial society, if often unpleasant from hunger and disease. Village elders and chiefs were responsible for justice and order. Most of the villages produced only sufficient

Hausa chief from northern Nigeria.

food for their inhabitants, who built their own huts and depended on their immediate resources. This manner of life is known as 'subsistence'.

Economic changes

Some economic developments took place, but usually near the coasts. The French found that groundnuts could be grown in Senegal; cocoa, timber, coffee and bananas in the Ivory Coast; that the palms of Dahomey would yield oil and other products. The British also began to grow groundnuts in northern Nigeria and Gambia. Palm products reaped a rich harvest in southern Nigeria and Sierra Leone. The Gold Coast was the richest treasury of all. Not only gold, but manganese and bauxite were found here, whilst cocoa production became even more important.

This economic development was mainly confined to agricultural products. Unfortunately, it left almost every west

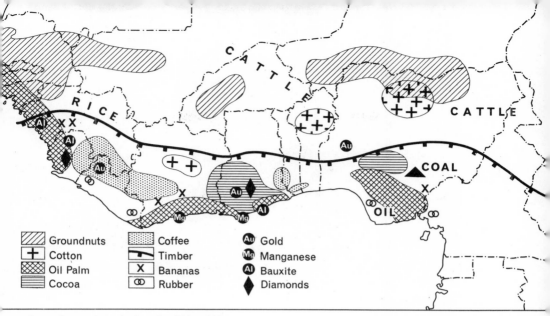

Crops, livestock, and minerals of West Africa.

African country dependent on the price which the world would pay for its export crop. The population was increasing, but scarcely any more food was grown for the people themselves. Even the railways and roads were built to the ports to carry export goods. Little was done to develop balanced economies so that each country could supply the needs of its people.

Some benefits were gained by west Africans. Increasing numbers of them took part in the production and sale of the main crops. Some of them acquired experience in commerce. And it was during this period that Britain and France began to offer government aid for development. This was small at first, but it pointed the way to the new idea of rich countries giving economic aid to poor countries.

During this period, too, the need grew for trained workers. This could only be supplied by greatly expanding the educational and training facilities available for Africans. In 1912–13 there were only 19,000 children at school in the Gold Coast. By 1956–57 the number had grown to 571,000; in Nigeria it increased during the same time from 22,000 to 2,020,000. These greater educational opportunities were often taken

D

Nursery of oil palms, Nigeria.

advantage of by young men and women who were later to become national leaders. They realized that education was the key to the power and skills which gave their colonial masters their strength. If the period was quiet, it was largely because Africa's young people were just beginning to think about and discuss the future of their countries.

Africans in politics

Few Europeans went to live in west Africa because the climate was so unhealthy. So there was little conflict over land ownership, and more Africans than elsewhere were allowed to participate in economic and public life. As early as 1871 Africans in the Gold Coast had begun to organize their own kind of government. The coastal states of the country joined together in a Fante Confederation. Their purpose was to resist the militant Ashanti from the interior. But they also planned to provide roads and schools, and to develop the country's resources. They were to have an assembly representing each of the 33 states, a government and a King-President. Unfortunately, the British mistook their intentions as anti-British and refused to recognize the Confederation.

In 1897 another political organization, the Aborigines' Rights Protection Society, was formed. In 1918, a famous African lawyer, J. E. Casely Hayford, founded the National Congress of British West Africa to demand greater rights for Africans in their governments.

The two world wars helped to increase African political interest. In both, African soldiers fought in many different countries, meeting new people and hearing many new ideas. After the first war, the German colonies, including Togoland and Cameroons in west Africa, were taken under The League of Nations' protection. They were administered on its behalf by Britain and France. This 'mandates' system brought the arguments about the morality and purpose of colonial rule into international discussion.

The Second World War influenced African affairs even more deeply. France was occupied by the Germans, and Frenchmen divided between the supporters of the Vichy government, which collaborated with the Nazis, and those supporting General de Gaulle and his 'Free French'. Most of the French administrators in west Africa preferred Vichy, but the Africans hated Nazi racialism. Eventually, in co-operation with French Equatorial Africa, west Africans joined de Gaulle. At a conference in Brazzaville in 1944 he promised Africans new political rights after the war.

It was during the second war, too, that the Atlantic Charter was proclaimed and the United Nations created. Their ideas excited Africans to new visions of their own right to freedom from colonial rule.

All these new ideas were more easily discussed because by now communications in west Africa had been greatly improved. Roads allowed more people to travel; newspapers, often written by editors with anti-colonial beliefs, were being read more frequently; the radio became another device for providing news of the outside world and stimulating discussion on the future of Africa.

The first stirrings of the new nationalism arose among the

educated generation which had grown up just before the war. In 1935 Nnamdi Azikiwe, a young Nigerian, returned from America where he had been studying at Lincoln and Pennsylvania universities. He began to publish popular newspapers which discussed Africans' political rights and were read by thousands of people. During the war he set up his own political party in Nigeria.

After the war discontent spread through west Africa. Soldiers returned to find few jobs available. Prices were high and goods scarce. Europe was short of machinery, so little was sent to develop African industry. Yet many Europeans went to Africa to earn high salaries. News of the independence of India and Burma, where many Africans had fought, increased the determination to attack the colonial system.

At this time Kwame (meaning 'born on Saturday') Nkrumah was in London. He had been a teacher in the Gold Coast and was inspired with nationalism by Dr. Aggrey, the first African member of Achimota College staff. Nkrumah then determined to study at the same American universities as Azikiwe. There he took part in American Negro activities. He began also to organize African students in that country.

Nkrumah was a very emotional young man. He felt very deeply the injustice of his people being ruled by foreigners. As he was leaving New York harbour he tells us:

> I saw the Statue of Liberty with her arm raised as if in a personal farewell to me . . . a mist covered my eyes. 'You have opened my eyes to the true meaning of liberty,' I thought. 'I shall never rest until I have carried your message to Africa.'

In 1945 Nkrumah went to England. He co-operated with George Padmore, a West Indian who supported African nationalism. They organized a Pan-African Conference held in Manchester. One of its chairmen was Dr. W. E. Burghardt DuBois, who had been a leader in the Negro and Pan-African movements since 1900. Another delegate was Jomo Kenyatta from Kenya.

The Pan-African Conference, Manchester, 1945.

This conference passed resolutions which included these words:

> The peoples of the colonies must have the right to elect their own Governments, without restrictions from foreign Powers. We say to the peoples of the colonies that they must fight for these ends by all means at their disposal ... Colonial and subject peoples of the world, Unite.

These words were a paraphrase of those addressed to the workers of the world in the nineteenth century by Karl Marx. Many colonial leaders considered that the struggle of the colonial peoples for self-government resembled that of the working classes for democratic representation in their governments.

Ghana

In 1947 Nkrumah took this message back to the Gold Coast. He returned to Accra to organize the United Gold Coast Convention. This party had been formed by some of the older nationalists, led by a lawyer, J. B. Danquah. In the year after

53

Students' party at Ghana University. Some of the men are wearing the traditional 'toga' of Kente cloth—made from long strips of brightly coloured handwoven cotton or silk.

Nkrumah's return growing discontent led to riots in Accra and other towns. The UGCC claimed that Britain could no longer govern the country and demanded self-government. An enquiry into the riots showed that they were caused by feelings of frustration amongst the Africans. It proposed that a more representative constitution should be introduced.

Next year, 1949, an all-African commission was set up under a judge, Mr. Justice Coussey, to propose details for the new constitution. Now Nkrumah took a decisive step. He broke with Danquah and the older, middle-class leaders who were working with Coussey. Condemning all compromise, supported by younger, more working-class enthusiasts, he formed a new party, the Convention People's Party. He demanded 'self-government now'. His party quickly became a popular, mass organization, with its own newspaper. It organized strikes and its leaders were sent to prison. They thus became martyrs in the eyes of their people.

Nkrumah was still in prison when the first elections under the Coussey constitution were held in 1951. Yet his CPP candidates were elected in most of the constituencies where direct voting was allowed. The governor, Sir Charles Arden-Clarke, wisely saw that he must work with Nkrumah or face revolution. So he released him and offered him the leading rôle in the new government. Nkrumah also chose co-operation rather than revolution. The two men became trusted friends.

Under this constitution the governor still held ultimate power. He and his chief officials remained in the government. Moreover, the majority of the legislative council members were not directly elected. They were elected from chiefs' councils or appointed by the governor.

Nkrumah now aimed to introduce universal suffrage, remove British officials from the government, and eventually transfer all the governor's powers to his government. This would bring complete independence. He believed that two factors would enable him to succeed. He and his ministers must prove that they could govern the country; and his party organization must carry the message of 'freedom' to the most remote villages of the Gold Coast.

So Nkrumah and his ministers rapidly increased education, built new roads and harbours, improved and organized the important cocoa production, provided better health services, and trained more Africans for the civil service. Above all, he had a vision of the whole country being transformed by building a huge dam on the Volta River to provide large supplies of electric power for new industries.

All this was not achieved without opposition. Nkrumah became Prime Minister in 1952; in 1954 the CPP won the first election held entirely on direct voting; the British officials withdrew from the government. But after the 1954 elections an opposition group called the National Liberation Movement appeared.

A model of the Volta Dam.

This consisted largely of conservatives, chiefs, discontented cocoa farmers, politicians and intellectuals. There was considerable violence for two years in Ashanti, the main centre of opposition. Attempts were made to persuade the British to disperse power from the central government to the regions before they left. The opposition group did not want to come under the complete authority of the new young men of the CPP when independence came.

But the CPP proved in further elections in 1956 that it commanded the support of most of the country. The British parliament passed an Independence Act. On 6th March, 1957, independence was proclaimed. The new state took the name of Ghana, from the ancient west African kingdom. The first black African colony had transformed itself into an African-ruled state. Africans throughout the world rejoiced. At the moment of triumph Kwame Nkrumah remembered the other Africans still under colonial rule. He declared:

Ghana's independence is meaningless unless it is linked with the total liberation of Africa.

Dr. Kwame Nkrumah on Independence Day, 6th March 1957.

Nigeria

The Gold Coast had taken the lead after the war in the political revolution which resulted in independence. This was partly because she was small enough to unify her people quickly; partly because of her comparative wealth. Her 7 million people had an average annual income of about £80; Nigeria's 55 million averaged only about £30.

a

b

Some people living in northern Nigeria.
(a) Hausa cattle drover in the north
(b) Moslems outside the mosque at Zaria, northern Nigeria
(c) Yoruba women
(d) Fulani woman pounding grain near Kano, northern Nigeria
(e) Ibo architectural student at Zaria University

c

d

e

But Nigerians followed not far behind. They gained similar constitutional advances as the Gold Coast. Their main handicap was rivalry amongst their different peoples. After all, they had only lived under the same government since 1914. Eventually it was decided to divide the country into three regions. The North was dominated by conservative Muslim rulers called emirs; the East by the lively, industrious Ibo peoples; the West by commercially-minded Yorubas. Each was given its own regional parliament and government. (In 1963 a fourth, Mid-Western, region was created.) They joined together in a federal parliament and government.

In 1960 Nigeria gained her independence. Nnamdi Azikiwe, from the East, became Governor-General and later President of the Republic; Alhaji Abubakar Tafawa Balewa, a northerner, was first Prime Minister. The size of her population and the wealth of her resources suggested that Nigeria would become the most powerful of all African states; but this would depend on whether national unity could gain precedence over tribal and regional loyalties.

Sierra Leone, a smaller, poorer country, became independent in 1961; Gambia, even smaller and poorer, in 1965.

During this same post-war period French West Africa was following a somewhat different path from its British neighbours. Whilst in 1945 Nkrumah and his friends were debating the tactics of African nationalism in Manchester Town Hall, French African leaders were in Paris. There they took part in the discussions on the new French constitution, as de Gaulle had promised. They were then allowed to elect members to sit in all the French parliamentary bodies. In addition, they were given their own councils in Africa, although French officials retained much influence and few self-governing powers were permitted.

The close association with Paris and French politics gave French Africans a common focus for their political activities. They formed a party called the Rassemblement Démocratique Africain (RDA, or African Democratic Convention). It had branches throughout the Federation of West Africa. Its leader was Félix Houphouet-Boigny of the Ivory Coast. But Senegal and her leader, Léopold Senghor, cold-shouldered it because of its early association with the French Communists. Senghor tried to build a rival group with the help of the French Socialists.

The progress towards independence in British west Africa eventually began to influence French Africans. They debated whether their future should be as part of a Greater France. In 1956, Houphouet-Boigny, now a minister in the French government, participated in drawing up a new law offering greater self-government to French colonies. Two years later de Gaulle returned to power. He introduced the new idea of a French Community. This would have left the colonies to govern their own internal affairs. External matters would have been determined in association with France within the Community. All French Africa, except Guinea, led by Sékou Touré, approved the new scheme.

But by now national independence, including membership of the United Nations, was becoming the popular policy of Africa. Guinea followed Ghana's example in 1958 and declared its complete independence. Senegal and French Soudan, temporarily linked in the Mali federation, demanded independent status in the following year. In 1960 the whole of the rest of French west Africa asked for and was granted independence as separate states. De Gaulle's Community never really left the drawing board. By 1965 every country in west Africa except Portuguese Guinea and Spanish Sahara was free from European rule.

4 East Africa

East Africa displays one marked contrast to west Africa. Its societies are more definitely multi-racial. In Kenya, Tanganyika and Uganda, Africans, Asians and Europeans live side by side. Many of the European and Asian families have made their homes there for three or four generations. They are not transient inhabitants like the managers, engineers or teachers of west Africa. They built their homes, farms, or stores to settle permanently. This feature has provoked most of east Africa's twentieth century problems.

By treaties in 1886 and 1890 Britain and Germany divided the eastern side of the continent between them. The Sultan of Zanzibar was the traditional ruler of these territories. But the two European powers shared his dominions between their own 'spheres of influence'. Britain took Zanzibar, Uganda and what is now Kenya. The Germans took the countries later known as Tanganyika, Rwanda and Burundi. Both Britain and Germany at first left the administration of these territories to private trading companies. Later their governments took control.

The Africans did not accept their new masters without opposition. In Uganda well-organized states had existed for several hundred years. At this time the most powerful was Buganda, beside Lake Victoria. In 1897 the king of Buganda, who was called the Kabaka, led his chiefs and people in revolt against British rule. They were quickly suppressed. In Tanganyika the Africans resented German rule, particularly the occupation of their land by German farmers, being forced to work for the foreigners, and the use of former Arab slave traders as administrators. Resentment rose to a violent climax between 1905 and 1907 in what was called the Maji-Maji rebellion. The southern tribes combined to try and drive out the

Some people of Kenya

(a) Arab in Mombasa

(b) Masai boy with cattle near Amboseli

(c) European from the Highlands

(d) Indian at Fort Hall

(e) Somali nurse from the northern frontier

Germans. They failed; the war cost about 100,000 African lives, as well as those of many Europeans, together with the devastation of vast areas.

Britain and Germany, however, brought some economic benefits to east Africa. The British began to plant cotton in Uganda in 1903. This crop was later to make Uganda comparatively rich. Later, coffee growing was added and copper mines started. The Owen Falls Dam, at the source of the Nile from Lake Victoria, now provides hydro-electricity.

The Germans also introduced cotton, coffee and groundnuts

Sisal drying in Dar-es-Salaam, Tanzania.

to Tanganyika. But the most important crop here was sisal, first planted in 1893. Much of the country's revenue came to depend on its export. The Germans also built some railways. Under subsequent British rule diamonds were discovered.

Asians and Europeans in Kenya

It was in Kenya that the major economic, social and political developments occurred. The modern history of Kenya really dates from the building of a railway from Mombasa to Uganda. This railway was considered essential for Britain to reinforce her position in Uganda —and thereby in the upper Nile valley. It was begun in 1896. Three years later it had reached 300 miles inland from Mombasa. Here a depot for railway construction later blossomed into modern Nairobi. This city became the centre of commerce, industry and the collection of agricultural produce. The railway tracks reached the shores of Lake Victoria by 1901.

Many of the workers needed for this engineering feat were brought from India. Those of them who stayed in the country, together with their fellow-countrymen who came to supply their needs, formed the Asian population of Kenya. (Another section of this community was drawn from the Arabs, long settled on the coast.)

Meanwhile, it was found that the interior highlands of Kenya were fertile and enjoyed an equable climate. They seemed suitable for European settlement. If Europeans could be attracted to farm the land their traffic would help to make the railway profitable.

The most effective leader of the pioneering European

farmers was Lord Delamere. He was a rich, eccentric, colourful Englishman, who gave up his English estates to experiment with tropical farming in Kenya. In 1914 he described his experience in these words:

> The result after a few years working was that sheep had proved a failure and big losses had been incurred; that the land had been proved unsuitable for improved cattle until the East Coast fever menace was dealt with; the wheat was proved to have come to stay. That the possibility of ploughing large acreages in a country where the plough had never been seen was proved to be an economic proposition: that large numbers of natives had been taught ploughing and working with other implements; and that I had managed to get rid of £40,000 in cash which I had invested in the country.

Others who followed him also grew coffee, sisal, tea and fruit.

It so happened that at this time much of this part of Kenya was almost deserted. Disease had struck both Africans and their animals. This led to a deep misunderstanding between European and African. The British government gave land to European settlers on 999-year leases. Sometimes a treaty was negotiated with a chief. The white farmers believed that the

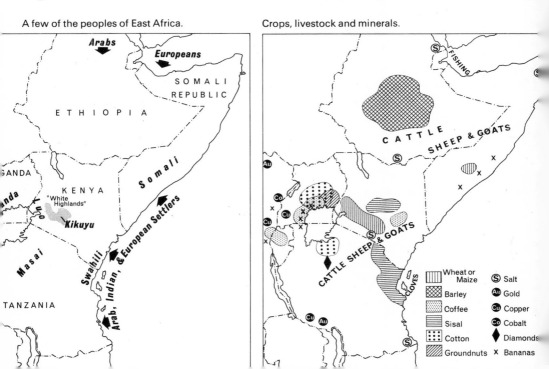

A few of the peoples of East Africa.

Crops, livestock and minerals.

land they were given belonged to them. But to the Africans, it was land permanently belonging to the tribe. Even the chiefs could not sell the land. Only its use could be leased temporarily.

These misunderstandings were to arouse bitter conflicts later. In the meantime, the European settlers, like those in other colonies, soon began to demand a share in the government of their new homeland.

An executive council to advise the governor was formed in 1905; two years later a legislative council was created. The executive was composed entirely of government officials. The legislative council included three nominated unofficial Europeans, together with the officials.

After the First World War a political battle was waged for control of the councils. But it was a battle first between Europeans and Asians. There were fewer than 10,000 Europeans and under 25,000 Asians in the country. The African inhabitants numbered several million. Yet it was the immigrant communities who were considered politically important.

The Europeans were promised eleven elected members in the legislature. Two unofficial Europeans and one Asian were to be included in the executive. The Asians demanded an equal number of representatives. This was really a fight between the two communities to gain control of the country. The Europeans aimed to develop it like South Africa, as a self-governing dominion ruled by themselves. Some of the Asians would have liked to see it become a province of India. After the Europeans had threatened armed revolt against the British colonial government in support of their claims, only five Asians and one Arab were admitted to the legislative council with the eleven Europeans. And each community was to elect its own members separately instead of all electors being on one electoral roll, as the Asians had proposed.

As a result of this conflict the British government decided that it must declare its policy for Kenya. The Duke of Devonshire, the Colonial Secretary, published a White (government) Paper in 1923. This came to be known as the Devonshire

Government road, Nairobi, Kenya.

Declaration. It included this statement:

> Primarily, Kenya is an African territory, . . . the interests of the
> African native must be paramount, and that if and when those
> interests and the interests of the immigrant races should conflict,
> the former should prevail.

But the European settlers remained wholly opposed to this
attitude.

Africans and the land

Meanwhile, some of the Africans were becoming aware of
these political developments. The Kikuyu tribe took the lead in
political agitation. Tribal awareness was stronger in Kenya than
in many other African countries, and European settlement
affected various tribes in different ways. Most of the land settled
by the Europeans was taken from pastoral tribes. The agricultural tribes found that they could not expand their farming
lands as previously. Yet, as a result of modern medicine, their
population was greatly increasing. So the same amount of land
had to feed more people and more cattle. At the same time, the
settlers demanded labour and often persuaded the government
to adopt measures virtually forcing Africans to work for them.

The Kikuyu lived next to the 'White Highlands', reserved

Kikuyu owned coffee estate

for Europeans. So they were constantly being reminded that the whites had taken land from Africans. Their reserve was also adjacent to Nairobi. So many of them became a minor part of European city life. This gave them more opportunities for education, training and political experience. But it also brought them up against the colour bar and often caused them to be unemployed. They were also spectators of the European attempts to gain control of their country.

During the First World War, many Africans served as porters in the army. Yet after the war, when they expected their services to be recognized, they suffered a new grievance. They were forced to carry a pass bearing their finger-prints, known as the 'kipnade'. They grew angry when they were prohibited from growing coffee and could see the Europeans making money from it on neighbouring farms.

One man came to represent all the mixed emotions of the Kikuyu people and those of other tribes who resented European privileges. His name was Jomo Kenyatta. He was born in the last decade of the nineteenth century and educated at a mission school run by the Scottish church. Then he worked for a time as a water inspector in Nairobi.

Kenyatta first became prominent in a struggle which revealed the double-sided nature of the Kikuyu outlook. It arose when the Scottish church demanded that all its mission teachers sign a declaration condemning the practice of female circumcision. This operation formed part of Kikuyu tribal tradition. Although some Africans, as well as Europeans, thought it cruel, Kikuyus strongly objected to European interference in tribal customs.

Kenyatta saw this issue as an opportunity to combine the tribal feelings of Africans with their modern demand for political rights. Many Africans broke away from European churches and formed their own. Independent African schools were also established. The Kikuyu Central Association, the main political organization of the time, enlisted many new recruits. Kenyatta became its leader and began to publish a Kikuyu-language newspaper to express African grievances.

In 1929 Kenyatta went to London to put the African case to the British government. In 1931 he went there again to state the case against the European monopoly of the White Highlands. This time he was to stay in Europe for fifteen years. There he worked, travelled, studied, lectured and wrote. His book, *Facing Mount Kenya*, explained Kikuyu customs and showed how African life was being disrupted by the Europeans.

During the second war the KCA was banned. But the first African, Eliud Mathu, was appointed to the legislative council. Up to this time a European had 'represented African interests' in the council. Europeans, whose numbers increased after the war when many people left Britain to escape from austerity, did not like the prospect of African political advance. They saw that now it was Africans, rather than Asians, who were beginning to challenge their power. By 1948 the Africans had increased their numbers in the legislative council to four, though there were still eleven Europeans. The settlers were becoming uneasy, particularly when they heard of Africans becoming ministers in west Africa.

Kenyatta returned to Kenya in 1946. Whilst in London he had worked with other African nationalists, like Kwame Nkrumah. He brought back knowledge of affairs in the rest of the continent and experience in modern politics. Like Nkrumah, he found much post-war discontent amongst his people. There were 10,000 unemployed in Nairobi alone, mostly Kikuyu. The KCA had been replaced by the Kenya African Union; as its name implies, appealing to all Kenyan Africans instead of only to the Kikuyu. Rather than take advantage of Kenyatta's experience and leadership, white society shunned him and government officials neglected to use his abilities. He set about building up the Kikuyu independent schools and became principal of their training college.

At this time Kenyatta was caught between two pressure groups. On the one side, some Africans were urging that only violence could stop the Europeans and convince the government of African rights. On the other were those who believed that advance by constitutional means was preferable.

The climax of the struggle between European and African claims came in 1951 when the British Colonial Secretary visited the colony. The Europeans demanded that they retain as many seats as those of all other races combined. They also presented a memorandum demanding a guarantee that

> African nationalism on the lines of West Africa was not Her Majesty's Government's policy for Kenya and that any statements which suggested such a thing was possible should be considered as seditious.

(This was the same year that Kwame Nkrumah and his colleagues had become ministers in the Gold Coast.)

The Kenya African Union (KAU) submitted a moderate programme to the Colonial Secretary. It suggested that it would be reasonable for the 5 million Africans to be given 12 members in the legislative council and that they should be elected; that people of all races be admitted to the electoral register; that Africans be given equality with other races in the executive; and that racial discrimination be prohibited. They also wanted greater educational and training facilities.

The Colonial Secretary tried to compromise. He offered Europeans 14 seats, Asians 6, Arabs 2, and Africans 6. So the European demand was conceded. But he also offered one African a seat on the executive for the first time. The British attempt at a compromise provoked disillusion amongst most Africans. They feared that their fate would resemble that of Africans in central Africa, where the white settlers were just being given domination in a new federation.

70

In 1952 acts of violence began to increase in the colony. It seemed that the 'violence' group was gaining control of African organizations. In October a State of Emergency was declared. Kenyatta and about 200 other African leaders were arrested. Six months later Kenyatta was convicted, in a somewhat unsatisfactory trial, for managing the terrorist organization, Mau Mau.

For the next three years civil war raged in Kenya. Africans, Asians and Europeans all suffered terror, mutilation and death. The war was fought mainly amongst the Kikuyu, many of whom took different sides and killed each other. The Mau Mau adopted bestial methods to enforce loyalty to their movement. Government forces were also guilty of barbarities. Civil war of this kind, fought in the villages and mountain forests, often between members of the same families, is inevitably brutal. It was ended soon after 1955 by victory for the stronger forces of the government, including both British and Africans.

One fact became clear from the Mau Mau war. It was obviously impossible for Britain to hand over power to the local Europeans. It had needed British forces and British money to meet the challenge of the civil war. Alone, the Europeans would have been helpless. But the British government was not yet prepared to give control to the Africans.

Multi-racialism or non-racialism

So, from 1954 onwards, various constitutional experiments were tried with the object of persuading the three main racial communities to share political power. Between 1954 and 1960 the British government was trying to ensure that members of every race were included in the government. This was known as 'multi-racialism'. It was rejected by the Africans. They insisted that members of the councils be elected as individuals, irrespective of their race. This was called 'non-racialism'. As there were far more Africans than all the other races combined, this policy would inevitably give the Africans political control.

In its efforts to impose 'multi-racialism' the British government tried a variety of methods. It limited voting rights by
laying down franchise qualifications; gave some votes more
weight than others; and insisted on dividing ministerial posts
between the races. All its efforts failed to satisfy African
nationalist aspirations. Once they had secured elections, the
Africans used them to publicize the demand for an increase in
the number of their members. They knew that they could
appeal to British democratic principles on the ground that
5 million Africans should have more representatives than
50,000 Europeans.

During and after the Mau Mau war KAU was banned,
whilst Kenyatta was still imprisoned in the far north. Two new
personalities now began to emerge. They were both from the
same tribe, the Luo, second only in size to the Kikuyu. It lived
in the west of Kenya and had not been implicated in Mau Mau.

Tom Mboya was a young trade union organizer who spent a
year in 1955–6 at Ruskin College in Oxford and some time in
America. He brought modern political experience to Kenya's
problems. Oginga Odinga, a teacher and business man,
represented the more traditional tribal outlook. The two men
sometimes worked together, but were always rivals for leadership.

By 1958, as a result of organized political pressure from these
two men and their followers, the Africans had secured an equal
number of elected members (14) with Europeans in the
legislative council. The more intelligent Europeans, led by a
farmer from Yorkshire, Michael Blundell, had begun to
realize that their hopes of power had gone. They even
acquiesced in forfeiting their monopoly of the White Highlands.

The way seemed open for radical constitutional reform,
leading, as elsewhere in British Africa, to self-government and
independence. But one vital issue still blocked the way. As it
became clear that Kenya was moving towards a more democratic system, demands began to be heard for the release of the

Jomo Kenyatta.

legendary hero, Kenyatta. He had served his prison sentence, but was still detained by government order.

The government was not yet prepared to allow Kenyatta his freedom. So, although leaders from all races agreed on a more advanced constitution at a conference in Lancaster House, London, in 1960, the problem of Kenyatta remained. One group of Africans refused to join the new government until he was free.

At this vital Lancaster House conference it was agreed that Africans should have a large majority in the legislature, with an African leader of government business. Some of the Europeans still protested, but their power had vanished.

Yet, after this conference, African unity disappeared for a time. Africans divided into two parties, the Kenya African National Union (KANU), which included both Mboya and Odinga; and the Kenya African Democratic Union, representing the smaller tribes against the Kikuyu and Luo. At the elections in 1961 KANU secured most votes and seats, but

top : Traditional homestead in Uganda.
above : New housing estate in Mombasa, Kenya.

refused to join the government until Kenyatta was freed. The pressure became irresistible. In August he was eventually allowed to return home, amidst tremendous rejoicing.

Kenyatta was still the national leader, despite his long absence in prison. Those who feared that he would impose Kikuyu domination on the other tribes were soon reassured. He tried to unite KANU and KADU, but failed. So he became president of KANU and tried to make it a national party appealing to all tribes.

In 1962 another conference prepared the way for fully democratic elections. When these were held in the following year KANU won a resounding victory. Kenyatta became Kenya's first Prime Minister. He formed a cabinet, including both Mboya and Odinga. After further negotiations with Britain, Kenyatta led his country into independence at the end of 1963. The man whom the white settlers had hated most, whom the government had blamed and imprisoned for the tragedies of Mau Mau, had become one of Africa's leading statesmen. Even the European farmers now regarded him as their surest safeguard for fair, orderly government.

President Nyerere of Tanzania, with an Indian shop owner whose property was damaged in a riot, 1964.

The drama of Kenya's struggles dominated east Africa during these years. Yet important developments were also taking place in the other territories. They were fortunate in that their smaller white settler communities never made strong efforts to gain political control.

In Tanganyika Julius Nyerere, a history graduate from Edinburgh University, quietly piloted his people to independence by December 1961. He was helped by the fact that Tanganyika was taken from the Germans at the end of the first war and placed under the League of Nations. Britain administered the 'mandate', which became a 'trusteeship' when the United Nations was formed in 1945. So Nyerere could always appeal to the UN when he was obstructed by the British government. But he really won his battle for independence by organizing his people into the first mass national political party in east Africa, the Tanganyika African National Union. Nyerere's TANU, like Nkrumah's CPP, proved that a well-organized national political party was the best weapon to break the bonds of colonial rule. His government, and that in Kenya, included Europeans and Asians, as well as Africans.

Uganda had more complicated problems to overcome. The ancient kingdom of Buganda remained her wealthiest province. It retained its semi-feudal structure, under the rule of its Kabaka. Economically and politically it was essential to integrate Buganda into the life of the rest of Uganda. But Buganda resisted. In 1953 the Kabaka himself was exiled to Britain for refusing to co-operate with the governor. He returned in 1955. But not until 1962 were these problems sufficiently solved to make independence possible. Milton Obote had become chief nationalist leader, and he agreed that Buganda should have special rights in a federal government. He became first Prime Minister and his agreement with Buganda allowed his country to gain independence in October 1962.

Zanzibar achieved its independence in December 1963. The main problem of these clove-growing islands, with their ancient, narrow, winding streets was the antagonism between Arab landowners and African workers. Soon after independence a bloody revolution overthrew the Sultan and the government. In 1964 Zanzibar united with Tanganyika as Tanzania.

By the end of 1963 all the British east African territories were independent. Together with the old kingdom of Ethiopia, and the Republic of Somalia, the new nations formed a solid block of African-governed states stretching from the Red Sea to Portuguese Mozambique.

5 Central Africa

The story of central Africa concerns two main areas; the Congo, which was ruled by Belgium; and the three countries governed by Britain—Nyasaland, Northern and Southern Rhodesia. Both areas are very different from west and east Africa in that they have considerable mineral wealth.

There are some other countries in this region. The four territories of French Equatorial Africa followed the pattern of French West Africa, whose story was told in Chapter 3. Like the west Africans, they became independent in 1960. Ruanda-Urundi, part of German East Africa, was mandated to Belgium after the First World War. It adjoined the Congo. On gaining independence in 1962 it divided into two states, Rwanda and Burundi. But it was in the Congo and British central Africa that the most important events occurred.

We have already seen, in Chapter 2, that the gold of Rhodesia and the copper of Katanga provided the foundations for medieval states in central Africa. We saw also that the first large African society encountered by Portuguese sailors in the fifteenth century was the state of Kongo, at the mouth of the Congo River. Yet Europeans knew little of these areas as late as the middle of the nineteenth century. It was the Arabs who carried the metals to the coast and who conducted the slave trade in this area. The Europeans stayed mainly on the coast.

It was the expeditions of explorers which brought central Africa to the attention of Europe. In particular, David Livingstone's hazardous journeys to the lands and rivers between the Atlantic and Indian Ocean coasts paved the way for others to follow into the heart of the continent.

Livingstone, a dour spartan Scottish missionary, found much of central Africa devastated by the Arab slave trade. He

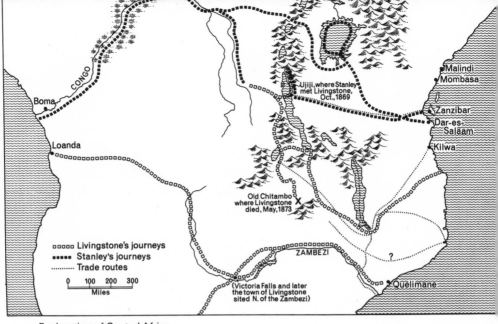

Exploration of Central Africa.

believed that it could be cured by a mixture of commerce and Christianity, bringing legitimate trade and a new morality. He wrote:

> ... if the slave-market were supplied with articles of European manufacture by legitimate commerce, the trade in slaves would become impossible.

And, in these memorable words, he begged people in Britain to sustain the interest in Africa which his travels had aroused:

> I beg to direct your attention to Africa. I know that in a few years I shall be cut off in that country which is now open. Do not let it be shut again.

Livingstone was followed by many Christian missionaries, especially from the Scottish Church to Nyasaland. His advice was heeded, for both a religious station and a trading company were started there. It is remarkable that, after the horrors of the slave trade, these early white visitors hardly ever encountered violence and were generally met with friendliness.

Yet, indirectly, Livingstone was also the cause of a development in central Africa which he certainly would not have welcomed. By 1871 his reports on conditions in these areas had

78

attained fame in the United States. The *New York Herald* sent a reporter to interview him. The young man chosen for this assignment was Henry Morton Stanley. He travelled from Zanzibar to Ujiji, north of Lake Tanganyika, to meet Livingstone. Stanley described the encounter like this:

> I came in front of the semicircle of Arabs, in the front of which stood the white man with the grey beard. As I advanced slowly towards him I noticed he was pale, looked worried, had a grey beard, wore a bluish cap with a faded gold band around it, had on a red-sleeved waistcoat, and a pair of grey tweed trousers . . . I did what cowardice and false pride suggested was the best thing —walked deliberately to him, took off my hat, and said: 'Dr. Livingstone, I presume?'

Stanley's expedition fired his own enthusiasm for African exploration. In 1874 he began to explore Lake Victoria and Lake Tanganyika. He proved that the former was the source of the Nile. Then he sailed down the River Congo to the Atlantic. When he returned to Europe in 1877 he was immediately employed by King Leopold of Belgium to explore the Congo further and develop trade in its basin. For his journey suggested to Europeans that there was great wealth to be gained in the Congo region.

The Congo under Belgian rule

Leopold was a very ambitious and greedy man. A Belgian historian wrote:

> From the high windows of his palace at Ostend he had allowed his imagination to run forth upon the waves.

In 1877 he himself wrote to a friend:

> We must lose no chance of securing for ourselves a share in this magnificent African cake.

Leopold persuaded the European powers to recognize his suzerainty over the Congo. He turned it into a private empire in which his agents practised appalling cruelties to force the Africans to produce rubber and ivory. A commission reported:

The successor of the murdered chief . . . attended by twenty witnesses, comes and lays a hundred and ten twigs upon the table, each of them signifying a murder for rubber . . . The soldiers had shown him the corpses of his people saying: 'Now you will bring us rubber!'

People in Europe and America organized protests against these shocking atrocities. Eventually, in 1908, the Belgian government became so concerned that it took the administration out of the hands of its king. The Congo became a Belgian colony. But the memory of these evil deeds perpetrated by white men on the Congolese lived on.

The Congo was a rich country. Its copper soon became much more important than rubber or ivory. It came to produce 70 per cent of the world's industrial diamonds. After the Second World War it also became an important source of uranium.

The Congo had its artists too. Their wood carvings, each tribe with its individual style, became famous in Europe.

The Belgians believed that their first duty was to help the Congolese to develop their own economy. They did not believe in teaching them politics. Powerful Belgian companies mined the copper and diamonds. They trained many Africans in technical skills. Christian missions, mainly Roman Catholic,

were encouraged to take educational and health services to the Africans. But almost all the education ended at the primary level and was mainly practical and technical. The literature of ideas, especially of political ideas, was not encouraged. The first university was not opened until 1954 and few Africans were educated overseas.

Yet the Belgians introduced relatively few colour bars into their colony. The number of European settlers was strictly limited. The cities were divided into European and African sections, but not very rigidly. More African children than in most African countries went to primary school and more Africans were admitted to skilled trades in the mines, industry or on the railways. In fact, it

Wooden figure from the north-east Congo.

Roman Catholic priest at a mission school in the Congo.

became the practice for African drivers and firemen to take their trains through the Congo to the frontier of Northern Rhodesia; there they had to hand over to white men, as only white train crews were allowed in Rhodesia.

The Belgian state, church and companies worked together to develop the wealth of the country and train the Africans to participate in the lower reaches of economic life. They hoped that an African middle class would emerge to co-operate with them. And perhaps, but not in the foreseeable future, Africans might eventually share the responsibilities of government.

In the meantime, no political activities were allowed for white or black. A Governor-General administered the colony. He was responsible to the Belgian Minister for the Colonies and a Colonial Council in Brussels. He had a council to assist him, but its members were nominated, not elected. Because there were no elections, political parties were not formed. So neither Africans nor Europeans took part in the kind of political activities which developed in other parts of Africa after the second war.

F

The Congo independent

This fact became of the utmost importance at the end of the 1950s. Suddenly, Belgian policy was reversed. All around the Congo's borders Africans were taking control of their governments. In 1958 General De Gaulle visited Brazzaville, in the French Congo, just across the river from Leopoldville. He gave the Africans there power over their own government. Belgium suddenly decided that she could no longer resist the tide of African nationalism. Two years later, on 30th June 1960, after a brief, hectic period of riots, conferences and elections, but with scarcely any preparation, the Congo was given its independence.

This sudden reversal of Belgian policy from absolute colonial rule to African independence brought disaster to the Congo. There were no African senior civil servants, doctors, engineers, economists, or army officers. The African politicians had had no chance of experience in government. They were left to rule their country without any of the educated, experienced colleagues who had helped ministers in other independent states.

It was not surprising, therefore, that only a few days after independence, the country fell into chaos. The army mutinied, turned on its white officers, and ran riot across the country. All forms of government almost totally collapsed.

At this time three men dominated the Congo's political life. Joseph Kasavubu was the President. He had been a government clerk, and was leader of the powerful Bakongo tribe living towards the mouth of the river. Patrice Lumumba was Prime Minister. As one British journal put it, 'M. Lumumba is a national leader; shaky perhaps, but there is no other.' Moise Tshombe, a business man, was President of the province of Katanga. He was supported by some of the Africans in this rich province and by the Belgians connected with the copper mines there.

In the years after independence Kasavubu and Lumumba quarrelled, whilst Tshombe set up Katanga as a separate state.

82

United Nations Troops in the Congo, December 1961.

The United Nations sent a military force to help to restore order and to compel Tshombe to reunite Katanga with the central Congo government. Lumumba was murdered and succeeded by several other Prime Ministers. After giving in to UN demands, even Tshombe became Prime Minister of the whole Congo for a time. He quelled a number of revolts with the aid of white soldiers recruited largely from Rhodesia and South Africa. This infuriated the rest of Africa, especially when the mercenaries were assisted by Belgians and Americans in rescuing white hostages.

By this time much of the country was devastated, its people suspicious of each other and inclined to turn back towards the safety of their tribes. Governments rose and fell, only Kasavubu retaining his position until he was replaced by the army commander, General Mobutu at the end of 1965. It seemed that it would take many years to unite the Congolese people and organize the state so that they could take advantage of the great wealth which their country provides.

Matabele defeated

The modern story of British central Africa begins with the influence of the ambitions of Cecil Rhodes on the Matabele and Mashona people in what is now Rhodesia. Rhodes was the son of an English parson who joined his brother on a South African farm, and made a fortune from the diamonds of Kimberley whilst still a young man. He sought new wealth to the north and sent his agents into Rhodesia in 1888. In 1889 he secured a Royal Charter from Queen Victoria and the Prime Minister of the day. He hoped that the gold reef discovered around Johannesburg extended northwards as far as the Congo. It was rumoured that gold, silver and copper had been mined previously in this area by Africans. (We now know that the rumour was true, as described in Chapter 2.)

At this time the Matabele tribe, which had been driven north from South Africa by the Boers in 1838, ruled most of present-day Rhodesia. Their king, Lobengula, was a massive, dignified man, nearly six feet six inches tall, and weighing about 300 pounds. He walked with his feet bare, his body naked but for a sporran of monkey skin, held by a blue belt. One French traveller wrote of him, 'I have seen many European and native potentates and with the exception of Tsar Alexander never have I seen a sovereign of more imposing presence.' He had inherited huge estates and about 500,000 head of cattle from his father, who had also bequeathed him a tribe with a high degree of military discipline. This had enabled the Matabele to dominate the neighbouring Mashona.

Rhodes's agents set out to persuade Lobengula to allow them to look for gold. After much hesitation and doubt, the king was eventually persuaded to affix his elephant seal and to sign his cross on a document for Rhodes which read:

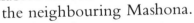

Lobengula, King of the Matabele; about 1893.

I, Lo Bengula, King of Matabeleland and Mashonaland and other adjoining territories, with the consent of my Council of Indunas, do hereby grant and assign . . . complete and exclusive charge over all metals and minerals situated and contained in my kingdoms . . .

But when white settlers began to appear in the country from South Africa and Britain and take possession of the land, the king and his people believed that they had been tricked. Both the Matabele and the Mashona fought against the occupation. They were defeated by the better-armed troops of Rhodes's Company, their social structure collapsed and they were henceforth ruled as conquered peoples. This is one of the few cases in Africa in which an African society was conquered by colonial invaders and its inhabitants ruled as defeated enemies.

Cecil Rhodes's overriding ambition was to see Africa from the Cape Colony to Cairo under British rule. Indeed, his dreams extended much farther. He once wrote a will in which he left his huge fortune to the Colonial Secretary to effect

. . . the occupation by British settlers of the entire continent of Africa, the Holy Land, the valley of the Euphrates, Cyprus, Candia, the whole of South America, the islands of the Pacific . . . the Malay archipelago, the seaboard of China and Japan, and the ultimate recovery of the United States.

The Colonial Secretary would have found himself with few people left in Britain!

It was as a part of this ambition that Rhodes established his British South Africa Company to prospect and trade. It ruled Rhodesia to the borders of the Congo and German East Africa. But north of the Zambezi the territory was gained by means of treaties with African tribes instead of by conquest. The peoples of Nyasaland, too, came under British rule in 1896 through treaties.

British in Central Africa

The British South Africa Company continued to rule the two Rhodesias until 1923. Nyasaland was governed by Britain as a

Protectorate. Some of the Nyasas also objected to alien rule. In 1915 a rebellion broke out against the British. It was led by John Chilembwe, who had been educated in a mission school and in America. He had met Negro protest movements in the United States, and some of them sent missionaries to Nyasaland. They believed that a 'Back to Africa' policy would help both the American Negro to get rid of discrimination and the growth of African nationalism. But Chilembwe's revolt was soon suppressed.

Despite this incident, on the whole relations between white and black were quite friendly in Nyasaland (Malawi). The Scottish Church provided many schools, so Nyasas found that they could get employment all over southern Africa. The Europeans were allowed by the Colonial Office to take only a little land, on which they grew tea, tobacco and cotton. Most of the Africans, except those working abroad, grew crops, tended cattle and fished in the lakes.

In Northern Rhodesia (Zambia), too, relatively little land was allowed to the Europeans though it was favourably sited. They lived mostly along the railway line which Rhodes built from Southern Rhodesia to the Congo. Some also settled in the north as ranchers or farmers. Many of the Africans had to live a nomadic life as the soil was so poor that they had to move from area to area to grow their crops.

But in the 1920s the copper of the belt along the Congo border began to be developed. This transformed Northern Rhodesia, which became the third largest copper producer in the world. (Only America and Chile produced more.) This development brought many more Europeans from Britain and South Africa to the Copper Belt and attracted even more Africans to work in the mines. The Copper Belt grew into a string of industrial towns inhabited by wealthy white miners and not so wealthy African workers.

It was in Southern Rhodesia that the rule of the white man was most evident. The conquering Europeans took half the land in the country for their own use. They enforced colour

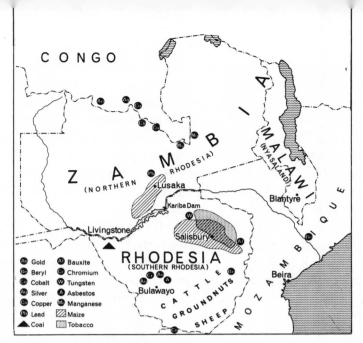

Countries and minerals of Central Africa.

bars, preventing Africans from using hotels, restaurants, public lavatories, separated housing areas, and insisted on Africans carrying passes, or identity cards. They became wealthy through growing tobacco, later mining and exporting coal, chrome and asbestos. The position of their two cities, Salisbury and Bulawayo, at the focal points of the railway system from north, south and east, encouraged the growth of commerce and industry. Many more settlers were attracted by this wealth and the luxurious life it provided; most of them soon regarded Africans as no more than servants.

In 1924 the royal charter which gave the British South Africa Company governing authority was due to expire. In the year before, the white settlers of Southern Rhodesia were given the choice of either joining South Africa or becoming a self-governing British colony. They held a referendum; by 8,774 votes to 5,989 they decided to become a British colony with responsible government. (At this time there were about 35,000 Europeans and 1 million Africans in Southern Rhodesia.) They were allowed to elect a Legislative Assembly, or parliament, from which was chosen an Executive Council, or government. The franchise was non-racial, but since few Africans qualified, voting was almost entirely confined to Europeans, who were given virtually complete authority over the affairs of the country, except that Britain retained responsibility for foreign affairs and some control over policy affecting Africans. The new white settler government, for instance, was allowed to raise its own police, army and air force. These forces were controlled by the Southern Rhodesian government, instead of, as in other colonies, by the British Colonial Office.

But the authority of the Southern Rhodesian government ended at the Zambezi. The northern territory now became the British Protectorate of Northern Rhodesia, under the Colonial Office; and Nyasaland remained in the same position.

From 1914 onwards some white people in the Rhodesias began to try to unite the two countries. At first most Southern Rhodesian whites were opposed to the idea. They thought the northern territory too backward. Then they feared that the Africans there were being given civic and economic rights too quickly by the British Colonial Office. But when Northern Rhodesia's copper began to be developed in the late 1920s, these objections seemed less important than the attraction of new revenues. From this time onwards, and particularly after the end of the Second World War in 1945, the two Rhodesias expanded rapidly as industrial countries. Coal, growing engineering industries, and commerce brought prosperity to the white community of Southern Rhodesia, whilst some Africans acquired wages as workers. In Northern Rhodesia a small, skilled, exclusive group of European copper miners were paid high wages, with Africans again providing the lower-paid labour.

Ten years of Federation
Before the Second World War several British commissions examined the idea of merging the two countries; they all rejected it. But after the war pressure from the white settlers

increased in both Rhodesias. They were led by Sir Godfrey Huggins, the doctor Prime Minister of Southern Rhodesia, and Roy Welensky, the ex-heavyweight boxer, engine-driver, trade unionist white leader of the north. To the economic advantages of a union Huggins added: 'For some time to come, Africans must be ruled by a benevolent aristocracy.' In 1950 the two men persuaded the British government to begin another inquiry, this time by Colonial office and Southern Rhodesian officials. The following year it produced a scheme for a federation of the two Rhodesias and Nyasaland.

Most Europeans thought that this scheme provided the opportunity for building a powerful new British state in central Africa. Some in Southern Rhodesia were against it. They would have preferred to go the South African way and were frightened that association with the north would help the progress of African nationalism. Some Europeans in Northern Rhodesia resented sharing their copper wealth with the south.

All articulate Africans in each of the three territories were bitterly opposed to federation. They saw in it an extension of Southern Rhodesia's discriminatory practices to the northern territories and the permanent imposition of white settler rule. They felt that giving the minority white settlers control over the majority African communities affronted human dignity and democratic rights.

But in 1953, by an Act of the British parliament, the Federation of Rhodesia and Nyasaland was created. Its parliament consisted of 35 members drawn from the three territories. Yet, although there were over 6 million Africans and only about 200,000 Europeans in the Federation, 26 members represented Europeans and only 9 the Africans. As Huggins was to explain later:

We want to indicate to the Africans that provision is made for them to have a place in the sun, as things go along. But we have not the slightest intention of letting them control things until they have proved themselves, and perhaps not even then. That will depend on our grand-children.

Mining Copper in Zambia.

Huggins was always blunt, saying honestly what he believed, however much it embarrassed those who were pretending that there was no discrimination. The policy of the Federation was supposed to be based on racial 'partnership'; Huggins again cut through this hypocrisy by describing it as the partnership of rider and horse—with the European as the rider.

The Federation was given authority over certain affairs common to all the territories. Local matters remained with the councils in the separate territories. So there were four parliaments, one for each unit and one for the Federation. Britain retained her responsibility as 'protector' of the northern territories; and an African Affairs Board was supposed to prevent racial discrimination, but never succeeded in doing so.

For the first few years the Federation was hardly troubled by African opposition. African Congresses, mass political parties, had been created in each territory—in Nyasaland in 1944, in Southern Rhodesia in 1946, and in Northern Rhodesia in 1948. In addition, the Africans organized a number of trade unions in the two Rhodesias. One of the strongest trade unions in the continent was the African Mineworkers' Union, under the leadership of Lawrence Katilungu, on the Copper Belt. It was organized with the help of a British trade unionist sent out by the Labour government. But the political parties were loosely organized and needed time before they could challenge the white-dominated Federation; the unions were busy raising wages and fighting against discrimination in mining jobs.

It was from 1956 onwards that African opposition began to become militant. Harry Nkumbula, who had attended London University, led his Northern Rhodesia Congress in a series of boycotts against the colour bar. Both the Northern Rhodesian and the Nyasaland Congresses now believed that they must fight the Federation if they were to save central Africa from following the South African path. They heard Sir Roy Welensky, the Federal Prime Minister, saying:

> It has got to be recognized, once and for all, that when we talk of maintaining high standards in the Federation . . . we mean White standards. People who have in their minds that we might abdicate in ten or fifteen years . . . ought to prepare themselves for a rude shock.

And they saw the British government giving increasing powers to Welensky's government. It seemed to the Africans that the time was now or never for them to avoid permanent rule by their white masters.

The climax came in 1958–9. In 1958 Hastings Banda returned to his native Nyasaland. As a youth he had walked to South Africa in search of an education. He eventually qualified as a doctor and practised in both London and Ghana. Despite his long absence, he had remained the accepted leader of Nyasaland Africans. Soon after his lieutenants called him back to his country he was demanding democratic elections and an end to Federation. Early in 1959 violence broke out, some Africans were killed, and Banda and his colleagues were put in gaol. At the same time an emergency was declared in Southern Rhodesia, where Congress leaders were also gaoled. In

(a) Dr. Hastings Banda, Prime Minister of Malawi.

(b) Kenneth Kaunda, Prime Minister of Zambia.

Northern Rhodesia a new leader had arisen to challenge Nkumbula. He was Kenneth Kaunda, previously secretary of Nkumbula's Congress and an admirer of the Indian philosopher-politician, Mahatma Gandhi. Kaunda was also sent to prison.

Welensky believed that these methods would crush African nationalism and that by 1960 he would be able to achieve full independence from Britain. This would have meant that a new state would have been created with the small minority of white settlers governing the 6 million Africans without any further British interference. But the open suppression of African nationalism was widely condemned in Britain. A government mission, led by a judge, Lord Devlin, described Nyasaland as a 'police state'. Later in 1959 Britain held a general election and Harold Macmillan was again returned as Prime Minister. But conditions in central Africa had been an embarrassment in the election. Macmillan now realized that if he was to continue supporting Welensky and his Federation there would have to be reforms. Otherwise Britain would become highly unpopular in a world where African states were now taking their places at the United Nations and in the Commonwealth.

So Macmillan replaced his Colonial Secretary, Lennox Boyd, a firm supporter of Federation, with Iain Macleod, who had more sympathy with African nationalism. At the beginning of 1960 Macmillan himself told the South African parliament that 'a wind of change' was blowing over Africa. In April of the same year Hastings Banda was released from prison. He reformed his Congress as the Malawi Congress and within a few months had reached agreement with Macleod. Nyasaland was to take the road of democratic progress.

The situation in Northern Rhodesia was tougher. There were many more Europeans living there than in Nyasaland. Whilst Welensky was prepared to lose Nyasaland, he had to keep Northern Rhodesia if the Federation was to survive. Macleod tried various expedients to get Africans and Europeans to share power. They failed. In the last resort, Kaunda's United National Independence Party and Nkumbula's rival Congress would rather work together than see a continuation of European rule.

The main question was whether Britain would allow those parts of the Federation ruled by Africans to leave it if they wished. Welensky thundered that this must never be allowed. Another commission, led by Lord Monckton, reported:

> The Federation is too much disliked to survive in its present shape . . . many Africans in Northern Rhodesia and Nyasaland look on Federation as a road-block in their path of constitutional progress . . . we recommend . . . immediate political advances in Northern Rhodesia and Nyasaland. We also make proposals to root out all forms of racial discrimination . . . under certain circumstances there should be an opportunity to withdraw from the association.

When the British government showed signs of agreeing with the commission, Welensky furiously accused it of treachery. He

The Kariba Dam on the boundaries of Zambia and Rhodesia.

declared that there were 'definite limits beyond which the white man will not be pushed', and asked his white voters for 'the sinews of war to fight with'.

Yet, by 1962, it was obvious that the Federation was doomed. All over the continent Africans were taking control of their own governments. The Congo, to the north of the Federation, had gained independence in 1960; Tanganyika, to the east, in 1961; Uganda, farther north, in 1962. Finding that the Federation offered them no prospect of equality, the Africans in the Rhodesias and Nyasaland inevitably demanded the same rights as their cousins in neighbouring territories. Nyasaland marched forward under Hastings Banda to become the independent state of Malawi in 1964; a few months later, Northern Rhodesia, led by Kenneth Kaunda, followed suit as the Republic of Zambia. The Federation had disintegrated under the pressure of African nationalism and was officially dissolved at the end of 1963.

Southern Rhodesia

This left the fate of Southern Rhodesia undetermined. The Europeans there, frightened at the increasing signs of African militancy around them, turned to open white nationalism. They were over 200,000 strong, with their own civil service, police, army and air force. In 1958 they had turned out their Prime Minister, Garfield Todd, for being too liberal. In 1962, although accepting a new constitution admitting Africans to their parliament for the first time (15 out of 65 seats), they replaced the comparatively moderate Edgar Whitehead with Winston Field, pledged to defend white leadership. In 1964 Field was replaced by an even tougher Prime Minister, Ian Smith. He was determined to give Southern Rhodesia independence from Britain without reducing white power over the Africans.

Meanwhile, the African nationalists were being harried by all these governments. Joshua Nkomo, a railway trade unionist, had emerged as the main leader. But each party he formed was banned in turn. He was criticized as not being sufficiently militant and some of his followers broke away under the Rev. Ndabaningi Sithole. Then Sithole's party, too, was banned. Both leaders, and most of their lieutenants, were either imprisoned or kept in detention in remote areas.

Ian Smith was now desperately trying to persuade or coerce successive British governments to give him independence. Both Conservative and Labour governments refused unless he gave Africans more power and promised a straight road to genu–

A Rhodesian soldier.

ine democracy. For each part of the British African Empire had been given independence only when all its people had the vote and had expressed a desire for British rule to end. This was not the case in Southern Rhodesia. Indeed, the majority of the white inhabitants there believed that if they accepted such a policy their comfortable life would be destroyed by African government. So they refused to allow the vast majority of the 4 million Africans to vote. Many of the Rhodesian Europeans sympathized with the South African belief in racial separation and relied on the South African whites to help them.

On 11th November 1965, Ian Smith made a sensational announcement. He declared on the radio:

> Now therefore we, the Government of Rhodesia, . . . do by this proclamation adopt, enact and give to the people of Rhodesia the Constitution annexed hereto.

The constitution proclaimed Rhodesia (the new name for Southern Rhodesia) a sovereign, independent state. But only an Act of the British parliament could give a colony legal independence. So the Rhodesian government was doing what the Americans had done in 1776; it was taking independence illegally, in defiance of Britain. The British government declared the Rhodesian action to be treason, imposed economic sanctions and called on all members of the United Nations to refuse to recognize the Smith regime.

No state recognized the regime, but South Africa and Portugal continued to help the Rhodesians economically. At the end of 1966 Harold Wilson met Ian Smith in conference on a British warship, the *Tiger*. But Smith and his Cabinet rejected the proposed settlement. So the Security Council, at Britain's request, made sanctions against Rhodesia compulsory. Their success would largely depend on whether South Africa and Portugal could be persuaded or coerced to stop helping the Smith regime. Meanwhile, Harold Wilson announced that now he would not grant independence to the Rhodesians until majority rule had been established. This was, indeed, a struggle for the 'no-man's land' between white and black nationalism.

6 South Africa

The peoples who live in the Republic of South Africa originated in three different continents. The Africans, of course, came from the African continent, though many from outside the present boundaries of South Africa. The Europeans are descended from Dutchmen, Germans, French and British. Indians and Malays came from Asia. Only the Cape Coloured originated in South Africa, for they sprang from a mixture of the other races. So in Cape Town, on the slopes of the massive Table Mountain, in Durban, beside Indian Ocean tropical beaches, or in Johannesburg, amongst the yellow waste dumps of the gold mines, oriental saris mingle with European cotton dresses, black with brown or white skins, rags from the African slums with the expensive suits of wealthy Europeans.

It is the attitudes of these various communities to each other which have given South Africans their many problems. They go back 300 years. For it was in 1652 that the little Dutch surgeon, Jan van Riebeeck, was sent out with about 130 men and a few women to establish the first European settlement at the Cape. He was sent by the Dutch East India Company to establish a refreshment station for Dutch ships sailing to the East Indies. The minutes of the Company, dated 12th December 1651, stated the object of the venture:

> ... to establish a rendezvous on the shores of Cabo de Bona Esperance (Cape of Good Hope) in order that our passing ships may safely touch there to obtain meat, fresh vegetables, water and other necessaries, and that our sick may be restored to health ...

So Europeans have been living in South Africa for over 300 years. They naturally regard themselves as white Africans, with South Africa as their only home.

Cape Town—an eighteenth century engraving.

When the small Dutch expedition arrived in Table Bay it found the country around almost unpopulated. Only Bushmen and Hottentots lived anywhere near. The yellow-skinned Bushmen were hunters, hostile to the settlers, but no match for their weapons. The Hottentots, probably a mixture of Bushmen and Negroes, tended cattle. They soon came to terms with the Dutchmen, traded their cattle, and became their servants. In the third year after van Riebeeck's arrival, he allowed two of his men to marry African women; in the sixth year, the first slaves arrived from Angola; the following year, conflict broke out for the first time between the settlers and the native inhabitants.

The rest of present-day South Africa was sparsely populated, but some Africans lived there. At about the same time that Dutchmen were settling down in the Cape, various African Bantu tribes were moving south seeking more fertile land, thus increasing the African population. For over 200 years the story of South Africa revolved around the growth and clashes of these two communities—European and African.

The Dutchmen were joined by Frenchmen and Germans fleeing from persecution at home over their Protestant beliefs.

The community grew wider and some of the more adventurous began to farm and herd their cattle in virgin lands far from Cape Town. They came to be called 'Boers' (meaning farmers) and developed a local language of mainly Dutch origin called Afrikaans.

In the settlement itself some Europeans had begun to turn against mixing on easy terms with Hottentots and with the slaves, who now came from Malaya, east and west Africa. It was accepted that any slave baptized into the Christian religion automatically became free. And a good deal of inter-marriage between Europeans and non-Europeans had taken place. Their children were the ancestors of the Cape Coloured community. But some of the Europeans now began to resent the loss of their slaves, white women arriving from Europe objected to mixed marriages, and some people thought that Christianity should be reserved for whites alone. The seeds of the colour bar were being sown.

These seeds were to sprout even more rapidly amongst the farmers on the edge of the colony. For, in the eighteenth century, the spreading European and African farming communities met each other. As European farms advanced eastward and African kraals moved west, the two encountered each other on either bank of the Great Fish River in the eastern Cape. On both sides a frontier society grew up, with constant raids across the river to steal cattle or recapture those previously stolen. Fear of the African was added to the European's economic resentment over losing freed slaves, thus deepening the growing colour prejudice.

At the end of the eighteenth century, during the wars with Napoleon, the British took over the Cape from Holland to prevent it falling into French hands. This brought a new source of grievance to the Boers. For the British were in the course of abolishing slavery. They brought laws which applied to everyone, irrespective of race. And missionaries came with them, some of whom defended the rights of Africans and Coloureds.

Over the mountains of Natal—a drawing of the Great Trek.

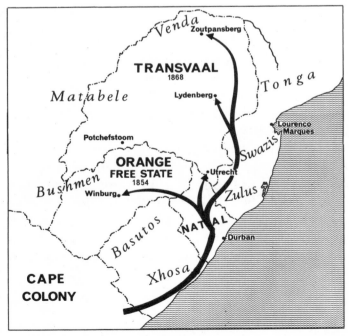

Some of the peoples of South East Africa, and the routes of the Great Trek.

After the final abolition of slavery in the British Empire in 1833, many of the Boers chose to leave the Cape. They protested against the principles and methods of emancipation. They formed expeditions composed of many families, each with its own ox-drawn waggon, and trekked away to the north and east to find lands where British rule could not reach them. Again they encountered African tribal communities, not now just the fairly amenable Xhosa (pronounced as nearly as possible in English 'Kkosa') of the Cape, but the warlike Matabele and Zulu. Many bitter wars were fought, but the spears of the Africans were no match for the Boers' guns. The Matabele were driven north, the Zulus east. The Basutos retreated into the mountains of Basutoland and, having asked for British protection, became colonial subjects as part of the Cape. The Boers took large areas of land and founded two new states, the Orange Free State and the Transvaal. In both, the principle, 'There shall be no equality in Church or State', was enshrined in the constitution. Meanwhile, Natal, where some Boers also settled amongst the British inhabitants, was annexed by Britain. For the rest of the nineteenth century there were frequent conflicts between the new Boer republics and the British government in the Cape, between Boers and Africans, and between the British and various African tribes.

Two discoveries transformed South Africa from a remote, unimportant part of the British Empire into a focus of international attention. In 1867 a man noticed children playing marbles in a Kimberley street. One of the little balls attracted his eye as brighter than the rest. The children gave it to him, and he sold it in Cape Town for £500. It was a diamond, and within months thousands of people from all over the world rushed to Kimberley to try their luck.

In 1885–6, the diamond rush was surpassed when gold was discovered in the Witwatersrand, a plateau 6,000 feet above sea level, where Johannesburg now stands. What had been open veld quickly became a series of rough, tough mining towns, and later the city of Johannesburg and its surrounding towns.

Johannesburg—in the background are the gold mine dumps.

The mining of diamonds around Kimberley quickly attracted both black and white labour to the area. But from the start the white workers insisted on a strong economic distinction between themselves and the Africans. All the skilled and semi-skilled, well paid work was to be reserved for whites; the 10,000 Africans who worked in the mines each year were only allowed to do the unskilled, poorly paid work.

This same pattern was repeated when gold began to be mined on the Witwatersrand. As these two great industries gave birth to new large towns, the urban inhabitants maintained the white master-black servant tradition of the countryside. In the twentieth century, as manufacturing industries developed, the same tradition was applied in them.

The discovery of these minerals radically transformed the South African economy. The Cape and Natal greatly increased their revenues from import dues on the heavy traffic passing through their ports. Between 1883 and 1895 the revenues of the

Transvaal Republic increased twenty-five fold from various taxes on gold. The Orange Free State also gained from the general prosperity. With much of the new money railways and roads were built, harbours improved, banks established, laying the foundations for a South African industrial revolution.

But the new conditions also brought problems. The new, vigorous, aggressive, mining communities depended on money and machinery. The older Boer society was based on land and cattle. It was a simple, God-fearing, rural society, thinking of little but its farms and the Bible. It felt itself threatened by the newcomers, just as in the past it had been threatened by the British and the Africans. The Boers had refused to admit Africans to the freedom they claimed for themselves; so now they refused to share it with the Uitlanders (newcomers) in the Transvaal gold fields. In 1895 there were seven Uitlanders for every three Boers in the republic. To give them equal voting rights would have seemed to the Boers like handing them their country. Yet those who came to the Transvaal to invest their capital and skill naturally demanded a share in government.

Two men dominated this conflict. On the one side, the Boers were led by the Transvaal President, Paul Kruger, a be-whiskered, obstinate, but homely old man, famous as a game hunter. On the other was Cecil Rhodes, son of an English parson, diamond millionaire, Prime Minister of the Cape, who was determined to create a united South Africa within the British Empire. He supported the Uitlanders and used his influence in London to involve the British government.

The British had been worried when the Germans declared a protectorate over South-West Africa in 1883. They then saw Germans, Dutch and Portuguese helping Kruger. Somewhat reluctantly at first Britain recognized the danger Rhodes had pointed out that foreigners might close the way north to British expansion. So the British annexed Zululand and Bechuanaland, whilst Rhodes secured a charter to develop Rhodesia. To the Boers it seemed that Britain was determined to surround their republic.

Rhodes destroyed much of his personal influence when he was implicated in an armed attack on Johannesburg led by his friend, Dr. Jameson, in 1895. The plot failed miserably, but it convinced Kruger and the Boers that the British intended to conquer them. They began to arm. The tension between the Transvaal and the British increased rapidly. In 1899 war broke out.

The Boers were defeated by 1902 and their two republics annexed by Britain. But this handful of farmers from the Transvaal, supported by their cousins in the Orange Free State, had defied the might of the British Empire and inflicted serious defeats on its armies. Even more important than the defeat, however, were the methods used by Britain to conquer them. As most of the Boer soldiers came from farms and used them as bases for attacks, the British eventually decided to burn down the farmhouses. They evacuated the women and children, sending them into refugee camps, whose conditions were so inadequate that 4,000 women and 16,000 children died there.

Thus, at the end of the war, the Boers were embittered not only by defeat, but by grief for their lost families and beloved farms. The grant of £3,000,000 by Britain for restoration did

Three generations of Afrikaners during the Boer War.

little to soften their resentment. Many of them determined to seek revenge; they resolved to rebuild the Afrikaner nationhood which they believed Britain had been intent on destroying since the 1830s.

It was Lord Milner, as governor during the post-war period, who succeeded where Rhodes had failed in bringing South Africa under one government. In 1906–7 the Transvaal and the Orange Free State were given self-government, though not full independence. In 1908 a National Convention of all four provinces met to discuss union between themselves. In 1910 a South Africa Act, passed by the British parliament the year before, came into force, establishing the Union of South Africa as a Dominion of the British Empire. This meant that the South Africans had their own parliament and government. But they were still subjects of the British monarch, represented by a Governor-General, and ultimate authority remained in the hands of the British parliament.

British opinion considered this to be a remarkably liberal settlement. For this was the age in which the 'rights of small nations' appealed to many British people. But most Boers—or Afrikaners as they were now called—still resented the defeat in war and were determined to destroy all British power over them.

Africans, Coloureds and Indians also felt aggrieved. It was all very well for the British to congratulate themselves on giving South Africans self-government. But the non-Europeans were quick to point out that this was self-government for only one section of South Africans—the minority with white skins. In a population of almost 6 million only $1\frac{1}{4}$ million were white; there were over 4 million Africans, half a million Coloureds, and 150,000 Indians. It is true that in the Cape voting rights had always been granted irrespective of skin colour. And these Cape rights were specially protected in the new constitution. But it was equally true that to vote in the Cape required educational and financial qualifications which could be gained by very few non-Europeans. And it was also true that virtually

a

b

c

d

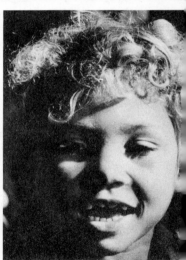

e

Children of South Africa.
(a) Indian   (b) Afrikaners   (e) Coloured
(c) Zulu   (d) Bantu

106

no non-Europeans in the other three provinces were allowed to vote at all. In fact, this constitution actually reduced non-European rights; they were no longer to be entitled to sit in parliament. (None had ever done so, but they had had the right.)

The few liberally-minded people—including the courageous W. P. Schreiner—protested to Britain. They saw the shadows of a future colour war. But their protests went unheeded. South Africa entered nationhood as a state of several communities all under white rule.

During the next 40–50 years these communities were engaged in two distinct conflicts. On the one hand, there was a struggle within the white community between those who would bring Afrikaner and British South African together and those who insisted that South Africa was primarily an Afrikaner nation; on the other, a battle raged between white and non-white communities over the issue of white domination.

The first struggle was largely dominated by two men, General Smuts and General Hertzog. Both had gained fame in the Boer War. But whereas Smuts was content to forget the past and unite Afrikaner with British, Hertzog demanded that the Afrikaner achieve equality with the more sophisticated British South African; and then insisted that Afrikaner ideas dominate South African life. (There were about 3 Afrikaners to every 2 British.) So Hertzog inspired a form of Afrikaner nationalism. It was marked by a campaign to secure equality for the Afrikaans language; to gain South Africa's independence from Britain as an equal member of the Commonwealth, symbolized by her own national flag; and to lay down the Afrikaner principles of strict Christianity, puritan morality and racial segregation as the foundation stones of the South African nation. Smuts was content to see Afrikaner and British contribute both their outlooks to a kind of coalition between the two cultures.

At first Smuts prevailed. He worked under the Union's first Prime Minister, General Botha, until the latter's death in 1919.

Then he became Prime Minister himself until 1924. During the First World War he became an international personality. But, as one of his biographers has written:

> Smuts had two completely different, even antagonistic personalities: the Smuts in South Africa, disliked and distrusted, impatient and easily irritated by administrative details, reserved and haughty to arrogance, often descending to political tricks and often petty; and the Smuts in England, the illustrious statesman . . .

After suppressing a strike of white miners in 1922 with such brutality that 800 were killed, Smuts was defeated by a combination of Afrikaner nationalism and white Labour at the next election. From 1924 until 1939 Hertzog remained South Africa's Prime Minister.

Hertzog presented a sharp contrast to Smuts. He was once described in these words:

> In the strong jaw and firm straight mouth one sees the dour fighter and true leader of the political masses.

And again:

> To him politics was not a game of tricks and intrigues, but a serious matter, almost a religion with which the fate of his people was bound up.

Hertzog had broken away from Botha in 1912 to found the National Party. (The first serious African party, the African National Congress, was also founded in the same year.) Once in power he put the principles of Afrikaner nationalism into practice. He secured equality for Afrikaans with English as a national language. At an Imperial Conference in London in 1926 South Africa and the other Dominions were recognized as 'autonomous communities within the British Empire, equal in status, in no way subordinate to one another . . .' He insisted that white workers be given preference in employment to non-whites and that non-Europeans should not be allowed to participate in skilled work.

Then came the world economic crisis in the early 1930s. Hertzog and Smuts joined forces to save South Africa from collapse and merged their parties as the United Party. Dr. Daniel Malan, formerly Hertzog's lieutenant, an ex-minister of the puritan Dutch Reformed Church, and a former editor of a Nationalist newspaper, refused to participate in the coalition. He took over the National Party and, with a few extreme nationalists, began to work for an Afrikaner republic and stricter racial segregation.

Many Afrikaners believed that Hertzog had secured all the objectives of nationalism with equality for their language and independence from Britain. But the extremists still suspected that Smuts and his British South African supporters were diluting pure Afrikanerdom. Hertzog and Smuts collaborated until the outbreak of the Second World War in 1939. But Hertzog considered that the war did not concern South Africa. He wanted to remain neutral. Smuts believed that the future of the Commonwealth depended on victory over the Nazis. He advocated support for Britain. By a majority of only 13 votes parliament supported Smuts. Hertzog resigned and Smuts became Prime Minister again. The extreme Afrikaners considered that this justified their belief that Smuts put Commonwealth before South African interests. They opposed him throughout the war and some, including Dr. Verwoerd, and Mr. Vorster supported the Nazis.

The final chapter in this story of the battle for Afrikaner nationalism was written after the war. Smuts had again become an international hero during the war itself. He had also participated in establishing the United Nations. But many Afrikaners still considered him a traitor to Afrikanerdom. In the first post-war election, in 1948, this section of Afrikaners was strong enough to defeat him. With a majority of only five, Dr. Malan was able to turn Smuts out of office and become Prime Minister. On the slogan of the Afrikaans word 'apartheid', which simply means separation (i.e. racial separation), an entirely Afrikaner government was formed for the first time. Those who believed in exclusive Afrikaner principles in South African life were now in a position to put them into practice. Smuts died in 1950 and his United Party rapidly became ineffective as an opposition to the Nationalists.

Through this period of struggle within the white community, the other conflict between white and non-white was continuing unabated. To understand it, we must retrace our steps. We have already seen that in the diamond and gold mines white workers were allocated the skilled, high-wage jobs and non-whites the unskilled, poorly-paid tasks. With the appearance of large-scale industry in the twentieth century, much the same practices were adopted. But some manufacturers modified the distinction, allowing Cape Coloured workers in particular a greater share of semi-skilled work.

The principal factor in the continued growth of colour distinction was the Afrikaner fear that South Africa's industrial revolution would undermine white supremacy. South Africa was an agricultural country until late in the nineteenth century. But much of its farming was poor. As it gradually improved to serve the needs of a nation becoming more urbanized, it could no longer afford to keep its many white idle, hangers-on, called 'bywoners', on the land. They, together with younger sons of Afrikaner farmers, found their way to the new towns, seeking employment. But they were untrained and often hardly literate.

In the towns these unskilled Afrikaners encountered Africans also looking for work. They, too, found that the land could not maintain them. The Natives Land Act of 1913 had allocated the African population only about 7 per cent of the country's total land area (increased to about 12 per cent in 1936), though Africans formed nearly 75 per cent of the population. In these Native Reserves most African families lived in small, round, thatched huts. They grew a little maize, raised a few chickens and tended their half-starved cattle. Their poor farming methods, like those of many white farmers, rapidly eroded the land. Only a small portion of the African population could sustain itself in these areas.

Traditional Zulu huts.

So Africans had to leave the Reserves. Some of them signed contracts for periods of labour in the mines, where they lived in strictly supervised barracks. Others worked in factories or as domestic servants for Europeans, often travelling long distances in the mornings and evenings from their tin and sacking shanties in the African townships. In these cases their land in the Reserves suffered even more, for only the women, children and old people were left to tend it. Other Africans found sustenance by living on white farms, the whole family working for the white farmer.

Whether it was on the farm, in the factory, on railways, in docks, or even on road work, the unskilled whites found themselves in competition for employment with Africans, Indians and Coloureds. Often the non-European, as a more docile worker, got preference. Most Afrikaners believed that if this was allowed to continue it would lead to a break in the convention that all white people must live on a much higher scale than any non-white. So all South African governments, whether led by Botha, Smuts or Hertzog, interfered with the conditions of employment to give preference to the white workers. They also tried to prevent as many Africans as possible from going to the towns.

In Sophiatown, Johannesburg. This area is now cleared and the people have been moved to a new housing estate.

The Africans tried to counter this discrimination by organizing trade unions. Some of these gained quite a large number of members during the 1920s. But many African workers came from other countries, attracted by an industrial society which, though paying low wages, gave them a better life than in subsistence farming at home. This increased the difficulty of organizing unions. They were no match for the white governments which refused to recognize them as bargaining organizations and frequently sent the police to break up their meetings.

The Africans also fought a losing battle on the political front. The African National Congress was formed in 1912. It became the main African political body and sometimes worked with the trade unions to try and stem the tide of discrimination. Its main test arose in 1936. For over ten years Hertzog had been trying to remove the African voters from the Cape electoral roll. Their right to vote alongside Europeans and Coloureds had been entrenched in the South Africa Act. By 1936 all qualifications for Europeans to vote had been abolished and European women had been given the franchise. But only

African men were allowed to vote and they had to fulfil the same qualifications as before 1910. This meant that Africans formed an even smaller percentage of the total electorate than previously. But Hertzog still wanted political segregation. He introduced a bill to separate the Cape African voters on their own roll which would elect three white members of parliament. The other provinces, where non-Europeans had no vote, would join with the Cape in electing four white members of the Senate.

Hertzog was able to get the two-thirds' majority he needed for this measure because he was supported by Smuts and his followers. The African National Congress and some other non-European organizations protested; but their protest was confined to demonstrations and had no effect on the government. Although articulate Africans, Asians, and Coloureds all demanded equality with Europeans, their efforts to secure it were ineffective. They were constantly harried by the white government, organization across the country was difficult, and they never solved the problem of mobilizing the masses for action. They found their rights continually diminished.

So, by the time of the 1948 election, the foundations of apartheid had already been laid. Land segregation, industrial segregation, urban segregation, and political segregation were already being practised. But there still existed certain trends in South African life which were undermining segregation. The Afrikaner extremists believed that Smuts and the British South Africans were encouraging them. Even though an economic gap separated white and non-white in commerce and industry, workers of different races were inevitably brought into personal contact in these occupations. Some of the more thoughtful employers even tried to break down the industrial colour bar to some extent. They would have liked to use their best non-European workers in more skilled jobs. Above all, it was continually obvious that the progress of the South African economy depended on an ever-increasing supply of African workers. Much of the white people's wealth, which provided

H

top : Aerial view of South Western Townships, Johannesburg.
above : View of the old (in foreground) and new Bantu townships.

New house at Temba.

New flats for Coloured people, Cape Town.

their fine houses, cars, servants and swimming pools, depended on African work. Yet this meant that more and more Africans must live in the towns, where they inevitably came into close contact with Europeans. The Afrikaner extremists would have liked the Africans kept right away from whites, lest the colour bar between them be broken down. Where non-white workers were needed, they insisted that it should be on the strict master-servant relationship of the farms, or within the rigid discipline of the mines.

It was largely the fear that industrialism, supported by Smuts, was weakening colour distinction, which led to Malan's victory in 1948.

Dr. Malan and his Nationalists were determined that apartheid must take precedence over economic advance. So they deliberately set out to use all their governmental powers to enforce segregation in every aspect of national life. Yet in the early stages there was no intention of completely dividing the country between black and white. As Dr. Jansen, who was to become Governor-General, put it:

> The presence of Natives in European areas, and also the fact that their presence there as labourers is essential, ... had been recognized.

The objective at this stage could be described in the Afrikaans word 'baaskap', or mastery. Johannes Strijdom, who was to follow Malan as Prime Minister, made this clear in a speech in which he said bluntly:

> South Africa can only remain a White country if we continue to see that the Europeans remain the dominant nation . . .

To accomplish this increased degree of segregation and to protect white rule the Nationalists had to take powers which interfered with white as well as black rights. They compelled everyone to register with the state, to be classified according to race. They forbad any form of sexual relations between white and non-white, within or outside marriage. They took powers to exclude anyone from public life, to detain them or to imprison them without trial. They prevented employers, especially in the mines, from providing family homes for their African workers. They made all inter-racial gatherings illegal. They decided where the different races could live and work. Yet, despite every attempt to keep white and non-white apart, the number of Africans in the towns, where contact was inevitable, continued to rise. The demand for labour still proved stronger than the desire for racial separation.

Africans, Coloureds, Asians, together with socialist, communist and liberal Europeans, all tried to oppose this flood of segregationist legislation. The African National Congress worked together with the Indian Congress, assisted by a few Europeans. In 1952, 8,000 people of all races went to gaol for deliberately breaking segregation laws. This non-violent protest was met by new laws imposing heavy fines, imprisonment and flogging. In 1956 the government arrested 156 leaders from all races on a charge of treason in what came to be known as the 'Treason Trial'. The protests did not deter the government. The Nationalists knew that the vast majority of Europeans supported segregation; the Afrikaners from conviction; the British South Africans because it seemed to safeguard their aristocratic way of life. Even the official opposition, the United Party, agreed with the segregation principle. And

An African priest with his pass.

the Africans, who had no votes, could only become dangerous if they were organized on a mass basis. Government security forces ensured that this would not happen.

There were a few Afrikaners who believed that apartheid would only become a just system if white and non-white were completely segregated in separate states. Whilst this looked fair in theory, it obviously could not happen in practice, for the South African economy demanded that black and white work even closer together. Yet this theoretical apartheid was taken by the Nationalists as a justification for extending their segregation policy in a new way.

It was under Dr. Verwoerd, the ex-professor of psychology and Nationalist newspaper editor who became Prime Minister in 1958, that planned segregation reached a further stage. Already all African education had been taken over by the state. This ensured that Africans were taught in their tribal languages, confined to tribal skills and excluded from modern knowledge which might undermine white rule. Now they were to be forced to accept that their Reserves were their only

Sharpeville, 1960.

homeland, even if they had always lived outside them. Dr. Verwoerd decided that a limited form of self-government should be established in the Reserves, starting in the largest, the Transkei, in the Cape.

We have seen how Hertzog and Smuts combined in 1936 to remove the Cape Africans from the electoral register, giving them separate (and white) representation in parliament. This was now abolished by the Nationalists, who also managed to remove the Coloureds from the electoral roll, leaving it completely white. Coloureds were given separate representation, as the Africans had been. All Africans were henceforth to accept that they must not consider themselves part of the South African state, but only of their own 'Bantustan'.

Elections were held in the Transkei, but the chiefs, who were responsible to the white government, were given a majority influence. The first government of the Transkei was led by Chief Matanzima who took the Nationalists at their word and said that all white men should get out of his country! But his government had only limited powers and remained under the authority of the white parliament.

Many people have forecast that apartheid, and the similar forms of segregation which preceeded it, would result in a revolution in South Africa. This has not happened and seems unlikely for a long time to come. The powers of the white-controlled state have grown enormously and have been unhesitatingly used against all opponents. In 1960, for instance, the police shot dead several score Africans at Sharpeville and in other areas where peaceful protests were being held.

In the face of this government use of force African organization continued to be ineffective. The African National Congress tried demonstrations, stay-at-homes, and strikes, but African trade unions were not recognized, and African strikes were declared illegal. Chief Albert Luthuli, President of the A.N.C., became world famous for his protests against discrimination and was awarded the Nobel Prize for peace. But the government removed him from his chieftainship and confined him to his farm. Frustrated by the lack of results, some Africans formed a

Chief Albert Luthuli.

new organization, the Pan-African Congress. Both it and the A.N.C. decided that non-violence was ineffective against the violence used by the government. They decided to organize a selected series of sabotage attempts. The government imprisoned their leaders. Nelson Mandela, who came to be known as the 'Black Pimpernel' from his many escapes from the police, was eventually captured. At his trial he made this moving declaration:

I have fought against white domination and I have fought against black domination. I have cherished the ideal of a democratic and free society in which all persons live together in harmony and with equal opportunities. It is an ideal which I hope to live for and to see realized. But if needs be, my Lord, it is an ideal for which I am prepared to die.

He was sentenced to imprisonment. Many opponents of apartheid, white, black and brown, were also imprisoned, often without trial. Some fled from the country.

It was not only the Africans in South Africa who tried to oppose apartheid. Most nations in the United Nations condemned it, though the protests were made in resolutions rather than in action. One action which succeeded was the demand of African members of the Commonwealth that South Africa be expelled from the organization. Their opportunity came in 1961. The Afrikaner ambition to break away from the British connection was fulfilled in that year, when a republic was proclaimed. But this obliged Dr. Verwoerd to ask Commonwealth members to recognize South Africa's new status. When it became apparent that they would not do so unless apartheid was abandoned, Verwoerd withdrew his country from the Commonwealth.

Another new factor appeared in 1966. Two of the three British High Commission Territories gained their independence, Bechuanaland as Botswana and Basutoland as Lesotho. The third, Swaziland, was expected to follow suit soon afterwards. This brought African-ruled countries right into the heart of South Africa.

The independent African states would have liked to organize a Pan-African campaign against white South Africa, if need be through a military invasion. They were particularly concerned at seeing the South Africans using their control over South-West Africa, mandated to them by the League of Nations, and building a defensive alliance with the Portuguese who governed Angola and Mozambique. Together with Ian Smith's white regime in Rhodesia, this seemed to raise a bastion, defending white supremacy throughout southern Africa against the march of African nationalism. But the South African military forces were stronger than those of the rest of the continent

Sir Seretse Khama receives the documents of independence for Botswana. His English born wife is with him.

combined. The most the African states could do was to help the African rebels waging guerilla war against the Portuguese in Angola and Mozambique, and to give some assistance to Africans training for revolutionary action in South Africa itself. In the meantime, they urged Britain to suppress the Smith rebellion in Rhodesia, demanded that the United Nations intervene in South-West Africa against South Africa's apartheid policy there; and hoped that eventually the great powers, the United States, the Soviet Union and Britain, would co-operate to abolish apartheid in South Africa itself.

7 Pan-Africanism

In 1945, when the Second World War ended, the only independent countries in Africa were Liberia, Ethiopia, Egypt and South Africa. The rest were ruled from Europe. Yet, by the end of 1966, 40 African states were independent. During this short period about 200 million Africans had been freed from colonial rule. Portugal still governed three territories, Angola, Mozambique and Portuguese Guinea; Spain one or two insignificant areas; South Africa and South-West Africa were still ruled by their white inhabitants alone; and the problem of representative government in Rhodesia remained unsolved. Nevertheless, during these twenty years African anti-colonial nationalism had won its major victories. It now found itself face to face with the strong white minorities of the south.

The political revolution which replaced colonial rule by African government created new problems for African leaders. In the first place the frontiers of these newly independent states had all been drawn by the European colonists. Often they cut through tribes, divided natural economic areas, ignored geographic regions. For instance, the Bakongo tribe was split between Angola and the two Congos; one part of the Copper Belt was in the Congo, another in Zambia; parts of Mount Kilimanjaro belonged to Kenya, others to Tanzania. Certainly the frontiers did not reflect national communities, for nations had hardly ever existed in Africa.

Yet the colonial rulers had governed the people within these frontiers as single units. So in their campaigns against colonial rule African leaders tried to organize a sense of nationality amongst the people within these units in order to agitate against their governments. They had certainly not converted the many tribal loyalties into national consciousness when

MADEIRA (Port)

CANARY IS (Sp)

MOROCCO 1956

TUNISIA 1956

SP. SAHARA

ALGERIA 1962

LIBYA 1951

EGYPT 1922 (UAR)

MAURITANIA 1960

MALI

NIGER 1960

CHAD 1960

SUDAN 1956

FRENCH SOMALILAND

SENEGAL 1959

GAMBIA 1965

GUINEA 1958

UPPER VOLTA 1960

NIGERIA 1960

ETHIOPIA

1960

SIERRA LEONE 1961

IVORY COAST 1960

GHANA 1957

LIBERIA

DAHOMEY

TOGO 1960

FERNANDO PO (Port)

SAO THOMÉ (Port.)

CAMEROONS 1960

1960 CENTRAL AFRICAN REPUBLIC

GABON 1960

CONGO 1960

REPUBLIC OF THE CONGO 1960

UGANDA 1962

KENYA 1963

SOMALI REPUBLIC

1963 RWANDA BURUNDI

TANZANIA 1961

ZANZIBAR 1963

COMORO IS. (Fr.)

CABINDA (Port)

ANGOLA

1964 ZAMBIA

MALAWI 1964

RHODESIA

MOZAMBIQUE

MALAGASY REPUBLIC 1960

SOUTH WEST AFRICA

BOTSWANA 1966

SWAZILAND

REPUBLIC OF SOUTH AFRICA 1961

LESOTHO 1966

AFRICA in 1945

Independent

British

Belgian

French

Portuguese

Italian

Spanish

Africa, April 1967.

independence was achieved. Thus there was always a danger that tribal conflicts could break out within the new states or that hostilities could occur between different states over border disputes.

The African leaders also recognized that political independence did not automatically bring complete freedom from colonialism. Most of the new states were desperately poor and had to depend on outside aid to give them a chance to build modern economies. But they feared that economic aid from America, Europe or elsewhere might be accompanied by political interference. They knew too that the colonialism which remained in the southern part of the continent was protected by strong military and economic regimes which could easily repel any attacks from the young, weak African-governed states.

Meanwhile, each new country had to establish relations with the rest of the world, by appointing diplomats, joining the Commonwealth or French Communauté, by becoming a member of the United Nations. There were obvious difficulties in finding enough trained Africans to take on all these skilled posts. There was the even greater difficulty of working out a foreign policy in a world beset by the Cold War.

The world looks a very different place from Africa than from America, Europe, or Asia. Africans do not think of themselves as Communist or anti-Communist. They are anxious to build new societies which will give their people the chance of a good life as the modern world understands it. They consider the Cold War to be other peoples' battle, meaningless to African needs. So they have tried to take the best from all systems of government and economics, adapting various methods to their own circumstances. They have been particularly frightened that friction between their new states or within these states could be used by each side in the Cold War for its own advantage. So they have adopted an international policy called 'non-alignment'. This implies that African states will judge every international issue according to its merits, not by considering the interests of either side in the Communist versus anti-Communist conflict.

The problems which faced the leaders of these new African states could only be met through co-operation between them.

If frontier disputes, tribal strife, economic colonialism, and involvement in the Cold War were to be avoided, Africans would have to stand together. And only such unity could give them a chance of defeating the white supremacy regimes of the south.

Some African leaders had realized the importance of African unity, or Pan-Africanism, as it was called, long before independence was in sight. A Pan-African conference was held in London as early as 1900. An American Negro, William Burghardt DuBois, attended this conference. He was to become the most famous of all Pan-African leaders, organizing many conferences and being chairman of the best-known, the Manchester Conference of 1945. Dr. DuBois died at the age of 95 in Ghana where he had eventually made his home. He and other American Negroes strongly influenced the Pan-African movement for they saw it as an important factor in gaining equality for all coloured peoples.

At the 1945 Manchester Conference many men who were to become leaders of the African revolution, like Kwame Nkrumah and Jomo Kenyatta, discussed how to defeat colonialism. The conference declared:

We are determined to be free . . . Therefore, we shall complain, appeal and arraign. We will make the world listen to the facts of our condition. We will fight in every way we can for freedom, democracy and social betterment.

These sentiments became the rallying cry for attacks on British, French and Belgian rule. On the morrow of Ghana's independence in 1957 Kwame Nkrumah claimed that 'Ghana's independence is meaningless unless it is linked with the total liberation of Africa'. At the end of 1958 an All-African Peoples' Conference was held in Accra attended by leaders of nationalist movements in countries still under colonial rule. Here national leaders like Kaunda, Banda, Lumumba, Mboya, discussed tactics to defeat the colonial powers.

African countries might have gained independence without creating a feeling of unity between them—just as happened in

South America. Some African leaders, however, always kept the importance of linking anti-colonialism with unity clearly in mind. Léopold Senghor of Senegal tried hard to keep the Federation of West African states together as the moment of their independence approached. He pointed out that such a federation would possess the resources and strength to mean something in the world, whereas his own little country of two million inhabitants could hardly exist on its own. Julius Nyerere declared:

> . . . the African national state is an instrument for the unification of Africa, and not for dividing Africa, that African nationalism is meaningless, is dangerous, is anachronistic if it is not at the same time Pan-Africanism.

In Ghana's independence constitution provision was made to allow the country to join with others in a Pan-African union. These African leaders saw unity amongst African states both as an international ideal and as a practical method of solving the problems they had to face after independence.

Those who were striving for African unity never thought of the Sahara as a barrier dividing their continent. Pan-Africanism extended to the whole continent, the Arab countries of the north as well as what is commonly known as 'black Africa' south of the desert. Indeed, there was always great concern for what was happening in north Africa. Egypt became a strategic area to European politics when the Suez Canal was cut in the nineteenth century. Britain took control of her because it was thought that the Canal was vital as a route to India and other imperial possessions in Asia. Various nationalist groups in Egypt tried to undermine British power over their country. But it was not until Colonel Nasser and some of his brother officers in the army took control in 1952 that British influence was finally ended. This was hailed by Africans as a triumph for anti-colonialism. When Nasser successfully defied Britain and France over the nationalization of the Suez Canal in 1956, Africans again felt that this was another victory over colonialism.

An Algerian is searched by French troops at a road block.

Algeria, Morocco and Tunisia had to wage even more bitter struggles to gain their independence from France. Nationalist wars against their French rulers were fought by each country. The Algerian war lasted eight years and was fought with terrible brutality on both sides. The ultimate victory of the Algerians over France and the European settlers of Algeria was regarded as another African triumph over European colonialism.

It was natural, therefore, that these Arab-African states of the north who had fought for and won their independence should play an important part in the efforts made to establish unity in Africa.

As we have seen, the idea of unity was discussed long before independence approached. Efforts to put the idea into practice began in the mid-1950s. In 1955 an important conference was held at Bandung in Indonesia. Here Africans and Asians came together for the first time to co-ordinate their ideas on international policy. It was at this conference that the principle of non-alignment was adopted by leaders from both continents.

Three years later, in April 1958, Kwame Nkrumah took the initiative in calling the first conference of independent African states. It met in Accra, and was attended by Ghana, Egypt, Liberia, Tunisia, Libya, Sudan, Morocco and Ethiopia. Already the number of independent African states had doubled since the end of the war. The conference was mainly concerned with discussing means for helping the remaining colonial countries to gain their independence.

In the same year another conference was held in Tanganyika to try and co-ordinate the anti-colonial strategy of east and central Africans. This conference set up an organization named the Pan-African Freedom Movement of East and Central Africa, often known by its initials, PAFMECA. Its original objective was to organize the nationalist struggle against British colonial rule in those areas and against the Central African Federation. But, from the start, its leaders discussed plans to build a great federal state under African rule to include Uganda, Kenya, Tanganyika, Zanzibar, Nyasaland, Northern and Southern Rhodesia—and, later, South Africa.

Julius Nyerere felt this need for unity particularly strongly. He believed that an East African Federation, later widened to include the central territories, would provide the most hopeful method of achieving it. He realized that if each state achieved its independence separately, many people would be reluctant to sacrifice their wealthy and powerful positions to enter a larger state. He also knew that once independence arrives a spirit of nationalism is fostered which makes it more difficult to merge the nation into a wider unit. So Nyerere actually offered to postpone the independence of his own Tanganyika until it could be attained simultaneously with those of Uganda and Kenya in an East African Federation. His offer was refused and his fears proved justified; after the three countries had become independent separately, efforts to federate encountered strong obstructions. But Nyerere showed his continued belief in the principle by uniting Tanganyika with Zanzibar in 1964 as the new state of Tanzania.

Nor did the rapid spread of independence from 1960 onwards produce immediate unity. Indeed, for about three years the continent was divided between two contending groups. Most of the French-speaking states formed their own organization at Brazzaville in 1960. This group, along with Nigeria, Sierra Leone, Somalia, Liberia, Togo, Libya and Ethiopia, then set up what was known as the Monrovia Bloc. It was countered by the Casablanca group, composed of Ghana, Guinea, Mali, Morocco, Egypt and the Algerians. Very generally one can say that the Monrovia states believed in a gradual approach to unity. They wanted to concentrate first on co-operation in specific functions, like telecommunications, airlines, customs and joint economic development. The Casablanca group wanted quick political union and were more concerned with radical social and economic reforms, getting rid of foreign economic control and building socialist states.

Just when it seemed that Africa might become as deeply divided as Europe, the African leaders turned back to the Pan-African path. In May, 1963, all African heads of state, except those from Togo and Morocco, assembled in Addis Ababa. There they set up the Organization of African Unity, designed to discuss policies aimed at uniting the continent whilst settling every African dispute in Africa and by Africans. The Charter of the O A U affirmed the 'sovereign equality of all Member states' together with 'non-interference in the internal affairs of States'. The object of the organization was 'to promote the unity' of Africa and to achieve 'a better life for the peoples of Africa'. The heads of state were to meet annually; the foreign ministers twice a year.

The creation of the O A U represented the apex of Pan-Africanism. It demonstrated African determination to regard the continent as a single international unit. It did not, of course, immediately remove all causes of friction. The leaders found that they could unite on the desire for unity, on non-alignment and on a determination to remove colonial and white settler rule. But, as in other continents, border disputes remained—between Kenya, Ethiopia and Somalia; Algeria and Morocco; Ghana and Togo; the divisions over the Congo civil war were still deep; whilst suspicions continued over rival political, social and economic ambitions.

These disputes severely strained the cohesion of the O A U in its early years. Africans were attempting to forge a continental unity never achieved elsewhere. And they were making their attempt in a period of revolution. As in other new societies, corruption, extravagance, inefficiency, intrigue appeared in African nations. Assassinations, mutinies, revolts overthrew many leaders and governments, increasing the sense of insecurity. Africans were searching for new forms of society which would preserve their own traditions whilst enabling them to transform their weak economies and to play a significant part in world politics.

This ferment was occurring just at the moment when Africa was emerging from colonial rule. The colonial period was only a tiny fragment of Africa's total history; but it coincided with the scientific, technological transformation of the world. Imperial rule, together with slavery, occurring at this crucial time, left deep scars. African society was totally dislocated, the continent left ignorant and isolated whilst much of the rest of the world enjoyed the benefits of the new age. Although Africa produced nearly all the world's diamonds, more than half its gold and a fifth of its copper, millions of Africans continued to live on less than £20 a year. Discontent, revolts and revolutions were inevitable in these circumstances.

Yet, despite all these troubles, as new regimes replaced old, Africans still held fast to the fundamental Pan-African ideals; full, equal political rights for all Africans; insulation from the Cold War; and a united African continent. The history of Africans in the future will be determined by the manner in which these principles are applied to the harsh realities of twentieth century international life.

For Further Reading

Roland Oliver & J. D. Fage, *A Short History of Africa*, Penguin 1962

G. W. Kingsnorth, *Africa South of the Sahara*, Cambridge 1962.

Paul Bohannan, *Africa and Africans*, Doubleday 1964.

Donald L. Wiedner, *A History of Africa South of the Sahara*, Random House 1962.

John Hatch, *A History of Post-War Africa*, Deutsch & Praeger 1965.

John Fage, *An Atlas of African History*,

Oliver, R. and Atmore, A., *Africa since 1800*, Cambridge 1967.

Index